managing
electronic
records

edited by **Julie McLeod**
and
Catherine Hare

facet publishing

Published by
Facet Publishing
7 Ridgmount Street
London WC1E 7AE

Facet Publishing is wholly owned by CILIP: the Chartered Institute of Library
and Information Professionals.

First published 2005

British Library Cataloguing in Publication Data
A catalogue record for this book is available from the British Library.

ISBN 1-85604-550-1

Typeset from author's disk in 10/14pt University Old Style and Zurich Expanded
by Facet Publishing.
Printed and made in Great Britain by MPG Books Ltd, Bodmin, Cornwall.

Contents

The editors and contributors

Xiaomi An is an Associate Professor at the School of Information Resources Management, Renmin University of China, Beijing, China. She received her PhD from Liverpool University Centre for Archive Studies in 2001.

Kate Cumming has worked in policy and operational areas of the National Archives of Australia and State Records NSW and was involved in the development of the NSW Recordkeeping Metadata Standard and the redevelopment of the Manual for Designing and Implementing Recordkeeping Systems (DIRKS Manual). She has conducted research into recordkeeping metadata and has recently completed her PhD on this topic. She is a member of Standards Australia's archives and records management committee, IT/21, and was a member of the allied ISO committee TC46/SC11. Kate is also involved with the Australian Society of Archivists' Committee on Descriptive Standards.

Judith Ellis is the owner and Managing Director of Enterprise Knowledge Pty Ltd. She has worked in the information and knowledge management field for over 20 years, throughout Australia and the Pacific, in consulting, recruitment, education and training. Judith has held various positions with industry groups and is a Branch President for the (Australian) Institute for Information Management, a member of Standards Australia IT/21 Committee, ISO Technical Committee (TC46/SC11), and a member of a State Ministerial Advisory Council on Public Records. She has contributed to a number of professional conferences and publications, edited three books, and is involved with a number of universities in teaching, course advice and development, and assessment.

Pierre Fuzeau has since 1985 has been a consultant specializing in project management in the field of knowledge management, electronic document management, internet and intranets, records management and archives management. He is currently chairman of the Serda Group, one of France's foremost companies specializing in information and knowledge management and records management. He is also publications director of the journal *Archimag* and its collection of practical guides (on electronic document management and records management). With the University of Angers, he was responsible for setting up the first French university qualification in records management and the first EDM project management certificate in France.

Catherine Hare is by training a records and information specialist and teacher with over 30 years' experience of working in information management in the UK and abroad, including a six-month contract at the United Nations in New York. She has undertaken consultancy and training contracts and helped to develop a Lifelong Learning Award for information and archives staff in the BBC and a Masters in Records Management by distance learning. She was joint editor of the *Records Management Journal* from 1994 to 2004 and Chair of the Records Management Society of Great Britain from 1998 to 2000. In her current post she is Manager of the UK Office of Community of Science, an American-based company that provides research funding and expertise services for universities and other organizations across the world, and she continues to work as a trainer and consultant in records management.

Verne Harris is Project Manager for the Centre of Memory at the Nelson Mandela Foundation. At the same time he is an honorary research associate and part-time lecturer in archives for the University of the Witwatersrand's postgraduate programme in heritage studies. From 2001 to 2004 he was Director of the South African History Archive, and before that he was a deputy director with South Africa's National Archives.

Hans Hofman is senior advisor at the Nationaal Archief (National Archives) of the Netherlands and co-director of ERPANET (www.erpanet.org). He is in this position involved in e-government projects and initiatives throughout Dutch government with respect to access and management of digital records and information in general. On the international scene he is involved in the Inter Pares 2 research project and in ISO TC46/SC11 as chair of the Working Group on records management metadata. Finally, he is researcher in the Delos 2 project on digital libraries with respect to digital preservation.

Thijs Laeven is senior partner of Innogration Management Consultants specializing in personnel and competency management in the world of archives and records management. He develops and implements pro-grammes for professional development, on and off the job, and lifelong learning for public and private organizations to support the organizational changes prompted by transforming information strategies. Recently he developed a standard professional and competency profile of the archivist, and he also contributed to the development of E-TERM and of a web-based competency profile generator.

Richard J. Marciano is Director of the Sustainable Archives & Library Technologies (SALT) Lab and Lead Scientist in the DAKS Group (Data & Knowledge Systems) at the San Diego Supercomputer Center (SDSC), at the University of California San Diego (UCSD). The goal of the SALT interdisciplinary lab is to develop information technology strategies and conduct applied research that will foster innovation in: digital materials and records collection and preservation; urban regional planning and develop-ment; and historical information science and computing in the humanities. He is principal investigator on the Persistent Archives Testbed (PAT) project, where data grids are used to study the automation of archival processes. Richard holds degrees in Avionics, Electrical Engineering and Computer Science (MS and PhD) and worked as a Postdoc in Computational Geography.

John McDonald is an independent consultant specializing in information management. During a career of over 25 years with the National Archives of Canada he held a number of positions that were responsible for facilitating the management of records across the Government. A particular focus was the management of electronic records. In 2000, he led an initiative jointly sponsored by the Treasury Board Secretariat and National Archives, which led to the report, 'Information Management in the Government of Canada – A Situation Analysis'. He has authored or contributed to government-wide guides and standards on the management of government information and has published numerous articles in leading information management journals. He is a past president and fellow of the Society of Canadian Office Automation Professionals, past chair of the Committee on Electronic Records of the International Council on Archives and founder and past chair of the Canadian Federal Government's Information Management Forum.

Julie McLeod is a Reader in the School of Computing, Engineering and Information Sciences, Northumbria University. She is involved in various innovative training and education initiatives for records management, including the Lifelong Learning Award pioneered with BBC staff, distance learning Masters and undergraduate programmes and bespoke training courses. She has undertaken a number of research projects in records management and is co-author of *Developing a Records Management Programme* (Aslib Know How Guide), editor of the *Records Management Journal* and a member of the editorial boards of the *Journal of the Society of Archivists* and the *Journal of Documentation*. She is a member of the BSI and ISO committees that worked on ISO 15489 and author of BIP 0025:2 (*Effective Records Management: practical implementation of BS ISO 15489-1*, London, BSI) on implementing the standard. Previously she had a long career in industry.

Reagan W. Moore is Director of Data and Knowledge Systems at the San Diego Supercomputer Center, where he co-ordinates research efforts in development of data grids, digital libraries and preservation environments. Research projects include the National Archives and Records Administration research prototype persistent archive, the National Science Foundation National Science Digital Library persistent archive, the California Digital Library Digital Preservation Repository and the Worldwide Universities Network data grid. Moore has been at SDSC since its inception in 1986, initially being responsible for operating system development. He has a PhD in plasma physics from the University of California, San Diego (1978).

David Ryan is Director of Records for the Royal Household. From 2001 to 2004, he was Head of Digital Preservation at the UK National Archives, where he led the team that won the 2004 Pilgrims Trust Award for Digital Preservation. Prior to joining The National Archives, David was Head of Information Management at Pfizer Ltd, where he successfully introduced a major change programme in the management of electronic records. He began his career as Curator of Maritime Records at Merseyside Maritime Museum. A graduate of King's College, London, he also holds a Postgraduate Diploma in Archive Studies from University College, London.

David O. Stephens is Vice President of records management consulting for Zasio Enterprises, Inc., a records management company based in Boise, Idaho, USA. He is the author of numerous books and technical articles on records management, and formerly served as president of ARMA International. He was inducted into the Company of Fellows of that organization in 1992. He has presented lectures on various records management topics in many countries throughout the world.

Preface

No records manager today would deny that managing electronic records is the biggest challenge that they face. This applies whether they work in the private sector or the public sector, in a large or small organization. However, managing electronic records is not only their challenge. The challenge also confronts IT managers and developers, because it depends on technology, and senior managers of the organization, because the information that records carry is a valuable and unique asset. It confronts middle managers, because they are responsible for implementing the policies and procedures to achieve the organization's goals; indeed, everyone in the organization faces the challenge, because the norm today is for each employee to have a PC on their desk to work with electronic records.

Managing electronic records is also a complex undertaking because it involves the creation, capture and organization of electronic records, and providing ongoing access to them. These records are very varied in nature; timely disposal must be arranged for those which have a fixed life, and long-term preservation for those records of historical value that need to survive over time. Finally, managing electronic records is a global phenomenon, although as yet countries in different continents are at varying stages of development in responding to the challenge, which continues to evolve as technologies develop and organizations change.

So, managing electronic records involves multiple roles, an extensive range of aspects covering the organizational, technical and legal issues, and ongoing exploration and investigation to achieve and share greater effectiveness and efficiency. To be successful, these all have to come together in holistic solutions, at the strategic and operational levels.

For this book we took as our starting point the challenge as outlined above. *Managing Electronic Records* is multi-authored and the professional expertise and backgrounds of the contributors reflect the multiplicity of roles needed to describe this subject. There are chapters from IT specialists; consultants, including one in organizational development; a managing director; academic researchers; and, of course, practising records managers. There are contributions from each of the five continents to reflect the truly global activity and developments in the field. As well as individual chapters on such key aspects as metadata, standards, digital preservation, ethics, legal issues and competencies, the book begins with an introductory chapter which outlines the challenge and proposes a top-level strategic solution. There is a chapter that reviews research in the field and, preceding the final chapter, there are two chapters that provide three case studies taken from the public and private sectors in different parts of the world. They describe and analyse practical implementations and share the lessons learned. In the final chapter we, as the editors, conclude with a proposal for a framework to move forward. This draws on all the chapters and addresses not only the strategic but also the tactical and operational dimensions in presenting a way forward.

Given such a diversity of subjects, stakeholders and nationalities it is not surprising that there are variations in preferred use of terminology across the world. This is the case with metadata, used in the singular in Australia but in the plural in the international standard, and recordkeeping versus records management. Recordkeeping, following the Australian lead, is now commonly used as an all-embracing term to cover the making and maintaining of complete, accurate, reliable evidence of business transactions, while records management is reserved for the processes established to manage the records produced in the recordkeeping operations. In this book we have adopted metadata in the singular and the respective definitions for recordkeeping and records management explained above.

Faced with such a huge challenge, the temptation either to focus on one aspect or do nothing is great. We hope that, by addressing not only the individual elements but also the holistic approach through the expert voices of our contributors, we have provided, for both students and practitioners of records management across the world, theory, insight, practical guidance and encouragement to analyse, design and implement systems and processes for managing electronic records.

To save readers having to retype the website addresses quoted in the text, a complete list of URLs is available on a companion website to the book at www.facetpublishing.co.uk/managingelectronicrecords.

Chapter 1

The wild frontier ten years on[1]

JOHN McDONALD

Introduction

Ten years ago I wrote an article entitled 'Managing Records in the Modern Office: taming the wild frontier' (McDonald, 1995). It focused on the challenges organizations were experiencing in managing their e-mail and other electronic documents in the unstructured office environment. This environment, common in most organizations at the time and, as this chapter will argue, still too common today, was one where business processes and workflow were not clearly defined, the user had relative autonomy over what information was created, sent and stored, and accountability for the management of information was unclear.

At that time I felt that the wild frontier was as temporary as the frontier the US and other areas of the world experienced back in the 19th century. In the early pioneer days ad hoc approaches to settlement and a rather chaotic approach to law and order gave way to a more settled environment where the rule of law and the means to enforce it were established. Responsibility for administering the environment was assigned and technologies (telegraph, roads and so on) were introduced to foster economic and social growth. In my naïveté I thought that it was a matter of time before the wild frontier of the modern office would evolve in the same way, spurred on by technology developments, new ways of organizing and designing work processes, and new techniques for making recordkeeping transparent and nearly automatic.

When I wrote the article I had naïve hopes and expectations of the technology that the future of recordkeeping was just around the corner. I envisioned a desktop where the icons on the screen would change to work driven icons supported by integrated workflow, wordprocessing, forms and routing software. It would also enable automated and transparent recordkeeping based on business rules developed for program managers by highly knowledgeable and skilled records managers and workflow/business analysts – all working together in harmony!!

A year or so later, Margaret Hedstrom (1997) reinforced this perception by explaining that there were others 'out there' who shared the same concerns as archivists and records managers about the management of electronic records and who were actively engaged in developing solutions. As far as I was concerned, with that kind of support and acknowledgement coupled with the growing expertise of the records management and archives professions, it was just a matter of time before we reached recordkeeping nirvana!

So here we are ten years later. Has the sheriff come to tame the wild frontier? Do we have a realistic view of technology and do we use it effectively? Are authentic and reliable records being generated in the office environment and being captured into recordkeeping systems? Have we reached the holy grail of recordkeeping where the right records are being generated, captured (ideally in a transparent manner), maintained and used in the right form at the right time for the benefit of the 'right' people (from program staff to archivists to the general public)?

This chapter suggests that, while significant steps have been taken, the path out of the wild frontier remains as elusive for most organizations as it was ten years ago. The chaos presented by e-mail and other electronic documents scattered around on C drives and unorganized shared drives remains as real today as it was ten years ago. And the frustration felt in not being able to find the right version, the critical briefing note, memo and so on, or to establish the complete story on an issue, or to cope with the growing mounds of diverse forms of information, is just as intense. The frontier of the modern office is still 'wild'.

There are reasons for this and there are also ways out of the wilderness, which this chapter seeks to identify. The chapter begins by exploring the changes that have taken place in the infrastructure of policies, standards and practices, systems and technologies and human resources required to manage electronic records in the office environment. This sets the stage for an explanation of why the wild frontier has persisted, offers some suggestions concerning how the pace of change might be accelerated, and explains why such accelerated change has become an imperative.

Infrastructure for managing electronic records

The effective management of electronic records is not just a technology issue. It requires an infrastructure of laws and policies, standards and practices, systems and technologies, and people, all supported by an effective management framework and leadership capable of continually aligning the infrastructure in support of the business of the organization. Over the past ten years the components of the infrastructure have experienced considerable change – some positive and some not so positive.

Laws and policies

In terms of recordkeeping *laws and policies*, for instance, some progress has been made over the past ten years in establishing accountability frameworks for the management of information including information in records.[2] New Freedom of Information (FOI) and privacy laws have been introduced and existing laws have been updated.[3] Evidence laws have confirmed the admissibility of electronic records[4] and new policies have been developed to guide the development of integrated approaches to the management of information (including information in records) (Treasury Board of Canada Secretariat, 2003). Increasingly such policies are being driven by business requirements,[5] in addition to requirements that focus on 'good' government, accountability and the public right to know.

It has been one thing to see records-related laws and policies developed but it has been quite another to see them implemented. The track record for policy implementation over the past decade has been poor. Major factors have included lack of resources, absence of strong leadership and, above all, poor understanding of what it means to design and implement records management infrastructures that are relevant to the new environment. The absence of strong, generally accepted and implemented policy frameworks, especially those that codify accountability for records and information, has been a major factor impeding the development of solutions that address the challenges presented by the wild frontier.

Standards and practices

Unlike the situation a decade ago, and as referenced in Chapter 2, there are numerous examples of *standards and practices* that have been developed by jurisdictions around the world to address the management of electronic records. The ISO Records Management Standard (ISO, 2001) (under revision) is a remarkable achievement that offers an excellent framework for establishing programs and systems for the management of records. The national archives of major countries as well as state and local archives and records programs have been very active in developing the tools and techniques to turn electronic records management into a reality.[6] Emerging open source standards, metadata models and digital preservation strategies offer the first hints that information interoperability across space and through time is possible.[7]

Unfortunately, similar to the situation for laws and policies, the pace of implementation has been slow. Why? It is not for want of recordkeeping standards. In large part it is because we have yet to gain an adequate understanding of how the modern office functions, how people collaborate, how decisions are made, and how information is generated, shared, used and maintained. Recordkeeping standards and practices will be difficult to implement as long as there is an absence of standards and practices for managing the way work is undertaken in the modern office.

They will also be difficult to implement if they are not placed within a broader information management context. The standards and practices employed by previously distinct disciplines such as publishing and communications (especially via the web), library services and records management are converging. The need to develop broad, multi-disciplinary approaches to metadata models and architectures is simply one of many examples that underline the fact that there are multiple but overlapping frontiers that need to be tamed. Nevertheless, collaboration across the information disciplines has been slow and silo-type approaches to the development of records management standards and practices have continued. These factors can only continue to impede progress in the development of standards and practices that are relevant to the needs of the increasingly complex office environment.

Systems and technologies

Over the past decade strong advances have been made in the development of *systems and technologies* that enable the effective management of electronic records. From automated records management systems for paper records[8] and the first research efforts back in the early 1980s,[9] to standalone electronic recordkeeping systems in the early 1990s, to their merging with document management systems in the late 1990s, to their incorporation into the mainstream products of major computer companies over the past few years, the evolution of these systems has been remarkable. Requirements definitions have become standardized[10] and various approaches to procurement have been adopted. Some organizations are even learning that successful applications are those where the systems have been mapped to one or multiple business processes.[11]

In spite of this progress, however, there have been far too many cases where electronic document and records management systems have been introduced simply as places where people can dump their e-mails, attachments and other electronic documents. Such cases typically fail. User resistance based on a lack of understanding of the benefits of the system, lack of user friendliness, lack of integration with other technologies, and inadequate approaches to classification and retrieval, inter alia, is often the chief reason for failure. Above all they fail because steps have not been taken to identify and define the work processes that would otherwise have provided a context and need for automated recordkeeping solutions. Compounding these factors is the general lack of expertise required to design the systems and integrate them into the modern office environment.

A related technology issue concerns the intranet. In the rush to develop easy-to-use, friendly portals to permit citizens and clients to access services and information, the enhancement of the public websites has been generating far greater attention than intranets. My mother has far greater access to government information and services than does the average government employee who is still facing a screen full of utility-based icons ranging from word-processing to e-mail. The vision expressed a decade ago of a screen supporting work-activity-driven icons supported by integrated software and work processes (supported by templates, automated routing and so on) reflecting automatic and transparent 'behind-the-screen' approaches to recordkeeping has yet to be realized.

Given the incredible technological changes that have taken place over the past ten years it is remarkable that the design of our desktops and work processes (if they can be identified at all) have remained essentially the same. And, after ten years, it is remarkable that we still have not invested the time and energy required to understand how the office functions and how it can benefit from advanced tools and techniques for managing work processes and the information associated with those processes.

Human resources

The absence of effective intranet environments supported by innovative approaches to work process design is one of the most important reasons why the vision expressed ten years ago has failed to become a reality. And underlying why this has happened has been the absence of skilled and knowledgeable *human resources*. In the vision expressed ten years ago, it was expected that a cadre of records management specialists would be in place to facilitate the development of the required infrastructure for managing information in the wild frontier. In some cases this has occurred. Competencies have been developed that were not around a decade ago.[12] Education and training providers have adjusted their curriculum with the expectation that more and more of their graduates will find their way into higher level and more influential information management positions. Course materials and teaching staff are in place in some institutions and jurisdictions that had not even been considered a decade ago.[13]

For many it has been too late. Organizations lost many records management staff in the 1990s as administrative budgets were cut and new computer systems (and their vendors) promised fewer cares. With the expectation that technology would provide the solution, most failed to invest in upgrading or acquiring the necessary knowledge and skills. The lack of e-records management capacity has been a critical factor in the inability of organizations to introduce the tools and techniques that would have otherwise addressed the challenges presented by the wild frontier.

Management frameworks

A decade ago, the *management frameworks* responsible for governing the infrastructure of recordkeeping policies, standards and practices, systems and technologies and people were often under a senior official responsible for administration. The concept of the Chief Information Officer (CIO) was still emerging and, just as is the case today, most were seen as technology officers rather than information officers. Today the CIO concept is still nebulous but on an increasing scale, information management (IM) programs such as library services, records management, web content management, data management and so on are finding themselves located under a CIO.[14]

One would think that such an assembly under a sole authority would raise the profile of records management and foster interdisciplinary approaches that would place records management in a broader context. The reality, however, is that most CIOs are struggling with what it means to build an IM program.[15] Few organizations have defined 'information management', established a vision of IM and, within the context of such a vision, developed a vision of what it means to manage records, especially within the context of the wild frontier environment of the modern office.

One of the major inhibitors to progress in the development of more advanced management frameworks has been simply the lack of understanding managers have of records and records management. One can't govern effectively something that one hasn't defined and doesn't understand.[16]

Leadership

These management issues could be addressed, however, if there was *leadership*. Leadership (and the lack thereof) is the single most important factor impacting the ability of organizations to move forward on the management of electronic records in the 'wild frontier'. In some governments leadership is beginning to emerge through the active role of central and lead agencies – a phenomenon that was relatively rare just a few years ago when few seemed to feel it was so important. In the Government of Canada, for instance, the Chief Information Officer Branch of the Treasury Board Secretariat has been working in partnership with Public Works and Government Services Canada and Library and Archives Canada to develop government-wide leadership to the development of strategies for addressing electronic records management issues. Senior level committee structures focusing on information management concerns are in place that were not there ten years ago. Other examples of collaboration and central agency direction can be found in other governments around the world.[17]

In too many cases, however, confusion over roles, responsibilities and strategic direction, coupled with a general lack of resources and expertise, have eroded the capability of these organizations to exercise a leadership role. The lack of understanding about electronic records and records management on the part of potential leaders is also a major consideration. Sometimes the role of an archives service can become an issue if it hasn't been clear about its objectives. Archives are logical candidates for the leadership role by virtue of the fact that they have a vested interest in the preservation of and long term access to electronic records and because they have developed the necessary knowledge and expertise.[18] However, the execution of their leadership role can be shaped in different ways dependent upon its objectives. If the objective of the archives in facilitating the better management of records is solely to secure the archival record then its strategies will take one perhaps narrowly focused form. If its objective is to support 'good' government while at the same time securing the archival record then its strategies will take another perhaps broader form. The lack of clarity on the part of the archives about its objectives can lead to confusion among the other lead players and inhibit the exercise of leadership that those living in the wild frontier are searching for.

All of these issues underline the fact that, while the frontier is no longer new (after all, the modern networked office has been around for some time), it is still 'wild'. For many organizations the reality still persists of out-of-control e-mail, information scattered all over C drives and servers, corporate amnesia, and a general lack of control and requisite leadership.

How the pace of positive change might be accelerated

Rather than end on a depressing (but realistic) note, however, I'd like to offer a few suggestions for how the pace of positive change might be accelerated. These suggestions focus on establishing a *vision*, enhancing *awareness*, assigning *accountability*, designing an *architecture*, and building *capacity*.

Vision

It may seem academic to say that we need a *vision* but, in the case of managing electronic records in the modern office environment, it is a fundamental building block on which everything else rests. In arriving at a vision of recordkeeping, however, it is important to build a vision of how the organization can be more effective in carrying out its mandate. This is a prerequisite to any vision of the underlying infrastructure and follows the principle that recordkeeping in the modern office will get better only if improvements are made in the way in which the modern office operates. Or, in other words, in addressing the management of records one should not start with the records. One should start with the processes that generate the records. In those areas where work processes are ill-defined and where program staff are experiencing significant problems in carrying out their work such a vision can be a catalyst to finding relevant solutions. It can also help an organization pursue significant opportunities that enable staff to take full advantage of the technology and information resources. It is only through such a vision that gaps in work process design can be identified and, from this, that initiatives addressing both work process design and associated recordkeeping can be established.

Awareness

A business-driven vision of recordkeeping is impossible unless those developing the vision and those who will be subscribing to it have an adequate level of *awareness* about recordkeeping concepts and the role records play in supporting the business and accountability requirements of the organization. The fact that many people still see records management as the management by file clerks of paper-based information no longer required to serve the immediate needs of the organization is a clear indication that much needs to be done to re-assert the importance of records and records management. In the modern office environment, little progress will be made as long as the records creators and users in this environment view records as the residue of their actions or as some administrative overhead.

Accountability

Accountability for the integrity of highly structured applications systems and for the integrity of the data generated in these systems is often much clearer than it is for the wild frontier environment where work processes are poorly defined and accountability for records may not be as clear. Guidance is required on developing and implementing accountability frameworks for records (ideally situated within broader accountability frameworks for information generally). Such frameworks would make clear distinctions between the accountabilities of program staff at all levels and the accountabilities of the records specialists responsible for establishing and maintaining the enabling records infrastructure (Canadian International Development Agency, 2001).

Architecture

We often speak about the need to develop new policies, establish new file classification systems or introduce new recordkeeping technologies to deal with the wild frontier but seldom do we assemble these components into an *architecture*. Such an architecture would ensure that the components of the records management infrastructure (policies, standards and practices, systems and technologies, human resources) are designed, built and maintained as an integrated whole within the business context of the organization. Good systems designers use a business-centred model to guide their architectural designs – so too should records and information managers. It is when a business model and the associated records architecture are jointly established that one can populate the components of the underlying infrastructure (knowing that those components will always have a business context). Finally, in ideal circumstances, the records architecture would form an integral part of an overall architecture for information management and information technology management.

Capacity building

The establishment of the vision, the accountability framework, the architecture and the underlying infrastructure require human *capacity* – people who have the required knowledge and skills to make it happen. In most organizations these individuals, especially those who could assume a leadership role, simply do not exist. If organizations are to migrate from the wild frontier they need to invest in specialists who understand recordkeeping and, above all, can help organizations improve the way they carry out their work. The eradication of 'organization and methods' experts has left a vacuum in terms of the expertise required to enhance office performance. Such a vacuum needs to be filled either by a new cadre of work process design specialists or by records specialists who recognize that work process design, business rule development and so on, must be addressed before effective recordkeeping can happen.

Needless to say all of this will have important implications for records management education and training providers, not to mention the development of strategies that must address a host of human resources issues such as job descriptions, job classification, training and recruitment, rewards and recognition, performance measurement and so on. The opportunity for the records management profession can be considerable because this extension of role into work process improvement might serve as a catalyst for migrating the profession from one that is perceived as clerical and operational to one that is strategic, standards setting and directly relevant to the business.

Towards a new vision

The pressure to accelerate the settlement of the wild frontier is increasing exponentially as society and organizations embrace the electronic environment. Ten years ago the web was still in its infancy and web browsers, the technologies that really helped to position the web as a viable instrument of business and pleasure, had only just been developed. Today the internet is pervasive and web-enabled services accessed through increasingly sophisticated portals are becoming central to the way in which members of society interact with one another and the way in which organizations shape themselves to provide improved services and remain competitive. The web-enabling of business functions and activities, such as those supporting e-commerce and e-government, are blurring the lines between the web, the highly structured applications systems environment and the unstructured 'wild frontier' environment as organizations strive to provide seamless information and retrieval services.

Increase in computer literacy

Over the past decade computer literacy has increased exponentially. From using debit machines, to playing games, to taking digital photos – people (especially young people) in all walks of life are becoming familiar with what it means to work with computers and, more importantly, with electronic information. People are creating their own electronic archives comprising e-mails, computer games, MPEG files and, more recently, digital photos. As these types of information objects augment more traditional forms of information, people are becoming more sensitive to the issues that office workers have been experiencing for years. How do I file these things? What do I name them and how do I describe what they are? How do I retrieve them when I need them?

They are also discovering the challenges of finding the valuable needles of critical information in the haystack of information that is returned as a result of a Google search. They are experiencing the same frustration about the information glut as the office worker. They are also becoming concerned about the issue of trust and reliability. How do I know I have reached a government site? How reliable is the information I have just accessed? Is it the right version? Is it current? Is it complete? These are the same questions that have plagued office workers for over a decade.

Within the office a whole new computer literate generation is entering the work force. Their expectations will be high that a trusted information environment will be in place to capture authentic and reliable information and to provide relevant, accurate and complete information as and when required. They will be less tolerant than members of the slowly disappearing 'wild frontier' generation, who, while frustrated, seemed to conclude that the challenges they faced were simply the cost of doing business. This new generation has heightened expectations concerning the ability of governments to manage information – on the one hand, from the perspective of the citizen expecting that the government can be trusted to manage the information supporting the online transactions the citizen is engaged in; on the other hand from the perspective of the employee expecting that he or she will be able to generate, use and maintain effectively the information that underpins the trust relationship.

This is a generation that is poised to establish a vision that will be much more advanced than the workflow-driven recordkeeping vision expressed ten years ago. What would such a vision look like (he says cautiously as a member of the previous generation)? Likely it will be rooted in the concept of the mobile worker who is concerned as much with relationship building as he or she is with their position in an organization. Cell phones, handhelds, instant messaging, laptops and desktops will be their tools and information in multiple forms from multiple locations will be the fuel that drives them. Web-based portals accessed via a variety of means will serve as secure gateways to a host of information sources and services – some local to the host organization and others spread around the world. Information access and retrieval will be seamless. More importantly it will be customized and often pre-prepared in anticipation of information requirements.

Customizing the interface

The interface will be customized for both the worker and the customer or citizen and the concept of an intranet separate from the internet or extranet will disappear. Citizens will be able to dip directly into the records systems of government agencies (subject to security restrictions) in order to scrutinize the conduct of government business (presumably just as government will have the potential to sweep across the personal financial accounts of individual citizens to facilitate, for instance, tax collection).

Records will be captured automatically based on predefined rules and integrated web-enabled workflow. Rather than being stored in central repositories, they might be distributed and managed in much the same way as scientists are using the unused computing power of home computers to perform complex calculations. So too could records managers employ the unused space of partner organizations (government agencies) to hold and manage valuable electronic records. Space management systems would move and migrate records among the various 'spaces' according to pre-defined criteria. Sophisticated software would ensure effective access and retrieval. According to such a model the archives would no longer need a repository. Archival records would have already been flagged and their management as archival records would have been looked after automatically.

Leadership

The achievement of such a vision of the future depends on the same factor that has had such an impact on the achievement of the vision expressed a decade ago. Leadership! Without leadership there can be no vision. Without a vision (founded in awareness and assigned accountability) it will be impossible to develop an effective architecture to guide the way forward. Without an architecture it will be impossible to develop the kinds of infrastructures that will turn a vision into a reality.

In the case of the 'wild frontier', if the records management and archives professions are unable to undertake the leadership role required then someone else will. And they will do so knowing they are simply dealing with issues that should have been addressed a decade ago – issues that, once resolved, will enable them to take the lead in the far more exciting task of building towards the vision of the future. It will be up to the records management and archives professions to determine if they want to be part of that new frontier.

References

Canadian International Development Agency (2001) *Accountability Framework for Information Management*, CIDA.

Hedstrom, M (1997) Building Record Keeping Systems: archivists are not alone on the wild frontier, *Archivaria*, **44** (Fall), 44–71.

ISO 15489-1:2001 *Information and Documentation – Records Management, Part 1: General*, Geneva, International Standards Organization. ISO/TR 15489-2:2001 *Information and Documentation – Records Management, Part 2: Guidelines*, Geneva, International Standards Organization.

McDonald, J (1995) Managing Records in the Modern Office: taming the wild frontier, *Archivaria*, **39** (Spring), 70–9.

Treasury Board of Canada Secretariat (2003) Policy on the Management of Government Information, Ottawa, www.tbs-sct.gc.ca/pubs_pol/ciopubs/TB_GIH/ mgih-grdg_e.asp.

Footnotes

1   The author is grateful to Andrew Lipchak and Hans Hofman for their valuable comments on earlier drafts of this chapter.

2   An example is the comprehensive *Accountability Framework for Information Management* developed by the Canadian International Development Agency, 2001.

3   There are many examples around the world of governments enacting freedom of information and privacy legislation from the UK, Canada and the developed world to Jamaica and other developing countries. The Canadian federal government's *Policy on the Management of Government Information* is an example of a comprehensive business-driven policy that embraces all forms of information (see www.tbs-sct.gc.ca/pubs_pol/ciopubs/TB_GIH/mgih-grdg_e.asp).

4   Evidence laws that account for the admissibility of electronic records have emerged in many countries. One example is the *Canadian Protection of Personal Information and Protection of Electronic Documents Act* (http://laws.justice.gc.ca/ en/P-8.6/index.html).

5   The purpose of the *Management of Government Information Policy* developed by the Canadian federal government is: 'to ensure that information under the control of the Government of Canada is managed effectively and efficiently throughout its life cycle. Federal government institutions must manage information in a privacy protective manner that supports informed

policy and decision-making and the delivery of high quality programs, services and information through a variety of channels and in both official languages.'

6 See examples such as the DIRKS methodology produced by the National Archives of Australia (www.naa.gov.au/recordkeeping/dirks/summary.html), the toolkits prepared by The National Archives of the UK (www.nationalarchives. gov.uk/electronicrecords/default.htm), the Canadian federal government's IM portal (www.tbs-sct.gc.ca/im-gi/im-portal/portal-portail_e. asp) and the '*fast track*' products and other information produced by the US National Archives and Records Administration (www.archives.gov/records-mgmt/policy-fast-track.html).

7 Some examples include Interpares (www.interpares.org/ip2_index.cfm), the Victorian Electronic Records Strategy (www.prov.vic.gov.au/vers/digitalarchive/) and the model presented in the Open Archives Information Systems (OAIS).

8 The functional requirements for electronic recordkeeping that were used in the FOREMOST and IMOSA projects in the 1980s were derived from a set of functional requirements for automated records management systems for paper records that had been developed by Jacques Malette of the National Archives of Canada in the late 1970s.

9 The 'Information Management Office Assessment' (IMOSA) project was a collaborative private–public initiative sponsored by the National Archives of Canada and the Canadian Workplace Automation Research Centre. The 'Formal Records Management Using Office Systems Technologies' (FOREMOST) project was a small pilot project involving the testing of prototype electronic records management software using a small group of users within the Policy Branch of the Department of Communications.

10 Examples include the US Department of Defense standard (http://jitc.fhu.disa. mil/recmgt/standards.htm), the MoReq standard produced by the European Commission (www.cornwell.co.uk/moreq) and the Records, Documents, and Information System (RDIMS) standard suite of software procured by the federal Government of Canada (www.pwgsc.gc.ca/rdims/).

11 One example of a growing number is the workflow driven electronic records management application developed by Agriculture and Agri-food

Canada; the application won a gold medal at the annual Government and Technology conference in Ottawa, Canada, 2004.

12 An example is the competency standard for the information management specialist produced by the Alliance for Library, Archives and Records Management (ALARM) (www.fis.utoronto.ca/people/affiliated/alarm/keypol.htm).

13 Examples include the universities of British Columbia (www.slais.ubc.ca/index. htm), Toronto (www.fis.utoronto.ca/index_MSIE.htm), Monash (www.sims. monash.edu.au/index.html) and Northumbria (http://online.northumbria.ac.uk/prospectus/coursedetail.asp? CourseID=178).

14 This may not be true for all jurisdictions but it has become prevalent across the Government of Canada.

15 One CIO explained that while he was pleased that all the IM disciplines now reported to him and that he understood intuitively the importance of bringing them together, he wasn't sure what he was supposed to do with them.

16 Several years ago a friend of mine told me that she had been walking down the hall when she bumped into a colleague who had just emerged from a meeting where senior executives were discussing the management of electronic records. When asked why she was shaking her head, her colleague explained that it was like listening to 10-year-old kids talking about sex – they were mature enough to know how important it was but not mature enough to know what it *really* meant.

17 Leading examples at the national level include the governments of Australia and the United Kingdom. In both cases leadership is coming from the respective national archives. Similar examples also exist at the level of the state (e.g. state of New South Wales), and the province (Government of Alberta).

18 In fact, according to two of the four ICA principles that were developed by the ICA Electronic Records Committee (www.ica.org/body.php?pbodycode=CER&plangue=eng) regarding the role of archives in managing electronic records, archives are expected to be involved in facilitating the establishment of policies, systems and standards and practices to support the life cycle management of the records required by government to administer themselves and hold themselves accountable.

And not only should they be establishing policies, systems and standards and practices, they should also be directly involved in their deployment through training, providing advice and so forth.

Chapter 2

The use of standards and models

HANS HOFMAN

Introduction

The topic of standards is one that is viewed ambiguously, certainly in the area of information and records management where they are not at the forefront. On the one hand people scratch their heads, because standards may not seem directly helpful to them and may restrict their autonomy, and on the other they are aware that some standards are needed to enable, for instance, communication and information exchange. Some standards in the current office environment are implemented almost naturally and mostly without much thought because of the software that is used or available. The Microsoft Office suite of software and the internet protocol TCP/IP are examples of widely used *de facto* standards.

The growing interconnectivity and interdependency of organizations in the digital world, however, increasingly require serious attention and thought by organizations as to the consequences for their ability to do business as well as the new opportunities offered. This is strengthened by the external pressure to provide access to information resources and to become open and transparent to the public. The world wide web would then be the main and in a way mythical and virtual place where all that information could be found. In trying to address those challenges one of the decisions organizations have to make is when and where they should or want to use standards. Such standards may range from quality assurance to information security to metadata standards, as well as records management.

This chapter provides a short overview of the world of standards, focusing on records and archives management. It is important for records managers to understand where standards come from, what different types there are and why they are useful. It includes a description of the most relevant standards, but this is not and cannot be exhaustive. One related area that is not discussed for instance is that of archives which, to date, has developed its own world of standards. Well-known examples are the International Standard on Archival Description/General (ISAD/G), ISAAR (CPF) and the Encoded Archival Description (EAD) and Encoded Archival Context (EAC). Those standards are not exactly related to records management standards, though they concern the same information objects.

The world of standards

Knowing where standards come from is helpful in understanding them. Different standardization bodies exist, formal and more informal, including the well-known International Organization for Standardization (ISO). The ISO is driven by national standardization organizations, which contribute to international (ISO) standards but can also develop national standards, for example BSI standards in the UK, ANSI standards in the USA and AFNOR standards in France. Other official international standardization organizations include the International Electrotechnical Commission (IEC), International Telecommunication Union (ITU) and United Nations Centre for Trade Facilitation and Electronic Business (UN/CEFACT), each responsible for different domains, but often with close mutual relationships. Standards published by these organizations are based on more or less formal procedures and are considered to be *de jure* standards. Another important source are communities that try to develop open standards, the main example being the Worldwide Web Consortium W3C (www.w3.org). Such standards are called open standards because on the one hand everybody can contribute to their development and on the other they are widely available and mostly at no cost. The main driver for such standards is a common need or concern in a community, such as in this case the issue of interoperability on the web. Finally, there are the *de facto* industry standards, such as Microsoft or Adobe's Portable Document Format (PDF). (A proprietary standard like PDF is now being transformed into an ISO standard, ISO 19005-1, which is intended to be a suitable file format for archiving documents.)

What is the value or meaning of each of these types of standards? ISO standards (apart from having to pay for them) are often rather theoretical and not always translated into or used in products, but they are based on international consensus and therefore have authority. Open standards seem to deal with both these problems, since they are developed by an international community, are often widely used in practice, have authority and people know exactly what they are about. As such they also have authority. The most telling example is EXtensible Markup Language (XML). *De facto* industry standards emerge because many organizations or people are using the products, giving them a good position and a lot of recognition. The problem here is that they are mostly proprietary. This means that their definition is not disclosed making it not only difficult to understand them but also making organizations dependent on the supplier. In practice, however, this is not a real impediment for using them. So it is often not the quality that determines what standards are used, but the reputation or the commitment of a community or the marketing, whichever comes first.

Mostly organizations will use a mixture of standards, thus enabling them to do business and communicate with others. In the information area this may include aspects such as information security, information resource discovery, geo-spatial data, digital preservation, interoperability of information exchange, scanned images, technical documentation, records management and so on and so forth. There seems to be no end. One of the problems is that many standards address similar or related issues, but approaching them from different perspectives. The resource discovery community, for example, is mainly interested in developing standards supporting accessibility and interoperability. The resulting Dublin Core standard, though, overlaps with records management metadata standards. The same goes for information security or preservation standards. Maintaining and preserving information (and records) in a secure environment is also a area of major interest in records management.

It is, therefore, very important for records managers to be aware of other standardization efforts and their possible interaction with records management interests. In organizations, too often different but complementary standards are considered and implemented separately. Co-ordination is necessary because organizations do not want to do things more than once. Standards should address their requirements in line with the business they carry out and if there are standards for different purposes, such as records management and information security, they should complement rather then contradict each other.

A possible approach in such a situation is to take one standard and identify the requirements as a kind of baseline and see what other requirements should be added from the other, instead of implementing them separately. This can be extended and applied to other related and overlapping standards as well. When those standards change, it can be dealt with in the same way.

It is important to take these considerations into account in order to make standards effective. It also stresses the increasing need for interdisciplinary approaches.

In short, standards on records management are not something on their own; they are or should be embedded in wider communities of standards. Influence, however, should be mutual. The records management community should, for instance, look at the information security domain, and in another area archives should pay more attention to how records management standards will impact on them. In practice, though, many records managers on one side and archivists on the other are still approaching them very much as separate domains.

Considerations for using standards

Although in many situations it may be obvious whether or not standards should be used, it may be useful to provide some arguments and considerations for using them.

Benefits of using standards include:

- supporting quality assurance, because standards set a recognized level of quality
- supporting information exchange and interoperability and as such increasing efficiency
- offering a framework for implementation, accountability and certification, because they provide a checklist of issues to be dealt with
- reducing costs, because they reduce unnecessary variety and support easier maintenance
- providing stability and authority because of international consensus.

Other considerations include:

- Standards may reduce flexibility.
- There are so many standards, how to know which one suits best?
- One size does not fit all in many cases, so adaptations to the actual situation may be needed.
- Standards may be too perfect (reflecting the ideal situation) or too abstract (because they try to cover all situations).
- Standards are not fixed and will change over time and thus require ongoing future maintenance.

Every organization has to decide what will prevail and where and when standards may or will support the business activities that have to be carried out. Each business sector has its own standards, for example engineering or computer technology, and in this context, the records management community has quite recently started to develop standards.

The remainder of this chapter examines some of the main standardization developments in the area of records management. Starting at the overarching, comprehensive level with ISO 15489:2001, standards for records management processes (functional requirements) and for the information needed to support authenticity, usability and reliability of records (metadata) are described. A special area for standards is the long-term preservation of digital records where there is a common interest with other domains such as libraries and scientific data centres. Here a reference model for a digital repository and many technical and structural standards such as file formats (for example PDF, JPEG and Word), mark-up languages, (for example HTML and XML) and data encoding (for example ASCII and Unicode) exist. Finally, two other related areas, information security and quality assurance, are touched on.

Standards in records management

Until quite recently there was hardly any international standardization in the area of records management. Most work was done based on practical experience and some shared understanding of what records management is or should be within a certain context, for example an organization, a sector or a country. This has changed.

An important driver for thinking and providing new approaches was the

Australian recordkeeping community. In 1996 they developed AS4390, the first ever standard for recordkeeping (Standards Australia, 1996). This was internationally received as an example that deserved further attention. The initiative was taken to establish an ISO subcommittee, TC46/SC11, to develop an international standard for records management based on the Australian example.[1] The result was the ISO 15489 records management standard, published in 2001 (ISO 15489:2001). Recordkeeping research in Australia also developed in the second half of the 1990s a whole new and powerful paradigm with respect to records, the records continuum, which has incited lots of discussion in the professional community (www.sims.monash.edu.au/research/rcrg/). Although not perceived by all records managers and archivists as such, it is one of the main concepts underlying development within ISO, because it is the only paradigm that allows the comprehensive, multidimensional view and approach that is needed in both a paper and a digital environment.

ISO 15489:2001 is the main and overarching standard for records management. It provides an excellent framework and a broad view of the principles and core issues. These principles will help organizations to assess and customize their records management needs for their business activities. The standard sets the scene in identifying and discussing the benefits of records management, the regulatory framework, policy and responsibilites, the characteristics of records and records systems, records management processes and controls, and monitoring, auditing and training. The perspective taken is that of the organization or any agent who needs to manage records in the context of doing business. The second part of the standard, ISO 15489-2, the technical report, shows how to achieve this using an implementation methodology derived from the Australian Design and Implementation of RecordKeeping Systems (DIRKS) methodology discussed below (National Archives of Australia, 2001)

Processes and functional requirements for records management applications

At a lower level a broad range of different sets of functional requirements for records management software applications have been developed. Some are standards, others are reference models. The main reason for this lies in the increasing need of organizations to implement software applications that support their management of electronic records. One has to be aware that to date none of them is really based on ISO 15489. They are mostly developed within other contexts.

One of the first sets was developed for the US Department of Defense, the DoD 5015.2 STD, 'Design Criteria Standard for Electronic Records Management Applications', issued as a standard in November 1997. It has already undergone a revision, which was released in June 2002, in order to incorporate, among others, the requirement to manage classified records, and is currently being reviewed again.[2] Because it was one of the first sets of functional requirements, and also because of the accompanying certification procedure, it has attracted a lot of attention worldwide. The Department of Defense requires software vendors to certify their software application against the standard, otherwise they it will not be eligible to be used. The standard has been translated into other languages and has served not only as an example for other sets, but also as the required set in tender procedures for records management software.

In Europe other sets of requirements exist. The best known is the set of Model Requirements for the management of electronic records (MoReq) developed for the European Commission and published in 2001 (www.cornwell.co.uk/moreq). It is a kind of reference model and is intended to provide a basis for organizations to develop a customized set of requirements, but can also be used for audit purposes. At the moment attempts are being undertaken by the DLM Forum to review and update the MoReq set. The current set is still too based upon UK records management practice and needs to be adjusted in order to give it a broader applicability, for instance in Europe.

The UK National Archives (TNA) has developed its own standard, last revised in 2002 (www.nationalarchives.gov.uk/electronic records/function. htm), and has run a programme for evaluating existing software applications against it, although it was announced in early 2005 that the programme will cease to be offered and the TNA's functional requirements will not be revised. A revised MoReq set may replace them. Examples of other sets of functional requirements are the Norwegian set (www.riksarkivet.no/english/electronic. html), the Canadian RDIMS (www.rdims.com/en/RDIMS.aspx) and the Indiana set (www.libraries.iub.edu/index. php?pageId=3313).

In summary, each set has its own history and background and, because of that, certain characteristics that have to be taken into account in order to identify whether such a set might be useful for an organization or not.

This is often not done, which might lead either to overkill – too many requirements – or to insufficient management with the associated risks. Another aspect that is relevant when evaluating these sets is their implicit or explicit metadata requirements. They have to be compared with the metadata requirements an organization may have, as will be discussed later. Furthermore, when people talk about functional requirements they limit them almost always to specifications for records management software. However, software does not work well if the procedural, organizational, juridical and business requirements of an organization are not identified and implemented too.

Finally, the number of existing sets can cause some confusion, not only for potential users or organizations, but also for the vendors, who may have to comply with all of them in order to compete in the market. There is not yet one international standard that has the right level of abstraction for everybody to use it as a reference model. It could be one of the tasks of the above mentioned ISO TC46/SC11 to develop this within the context of ISO 15489.

Metadata standards

Closely related to functional requirements is, as indicated, metadata. Here we are entering an incredible, complex and often bewildering domain. Though the term metadata is literally 'data about data' and does not really say anything, it gets its real meaning within the different business contexts in which it is used. Resource discovery metadata, for example, helps in improving retrievability and access to information sources, especially on the web. Preservation metadata refers to those metadata that support the preservation of digital objects. The main focus here will be on records management metadata.

In May 2004 the first standard, a technical specification identifying and describing the principles of records management metadata, ISO 23081-1, was published (ISO, 23081-1:2004). It will be replaced in 2005 by a slightly revised version as a standard. As indicated in the title it is a high level standard which explains what records management metadata is, why it is necessary, what roles and responsibilities can be identified, what types of metadata exist and how to manage them. The standard will consist of two other parts. In the second part a further explanation will be given on how to build and implement metadata schemas and the last part will provide a self-assessment instrument with which an organization can evaluate to what extent metadata schemas they have developed or chosen comply with the principles identified in the first part. In all, the whole set provides a solid framework for organizations to make decisions on the issue of records management metadata.

In the last decade several sets of records management metadata have been developed in different places, for instance in Australia at the national level (www.naa.gov.au/recordkeeping/control/rkms/summary.htm) and in New South Wales (www.records.nsw.gov.au/publicsector/rk/rib/rib18.htm# NRKMS), in Canada (www.collectionscanada.ca/metaforum/n11-232-e. html), in the UK (www.govtalk.gov.uk/documents/Records_management_ metadata_standard_2002.doc), and Minnesota in the USA (www.mnhs.org/ preserve/records/electronicrecords/ermetadata.html), but there are many more. Most of these sets are national or local and in their definition they may use ISO standards, for instance ISO 3166 for the country code (ISO, 3166-1:1997; ISO, 3166-2:1998; ISO, 3166-3:1999) or ISO 8601:2000 for the date structure.

Helpful for finding out about records management metadata sets is a metadata schema registry that describes metadata sets or schemas. It can be a great help in identifying and choosing these sets and schemas, because it contain descriptions that help to understand where they come from, why they were developed and what they are about. Another benefit of registries may be the possibility to compare the described standards and to do 'cross-walks'. The latter raises an issue, though, because metadata sets are not documented according to one standard. This often makes it very difficult to compare them.

A registry for records management metadata is currently being built under the umbrella of the InterPARES project, which will also support the evaluation of metadata sets against the principles of the ISO 23081-1:2004 standard and the requirements emerging from the InterPARES I project (www.interpares.org/ip2/ip2_description.cfm). This has been done for the metadata sets mentioned above, for instance, and gives insight into the strengths and weaknesses of those metadata sets.

Finally, the Dublin Core standard (www.dublincore.org) is often mentioned as a possible candidate for records management metadata. However, its purpose is to serve retrievability of web resources and it can be seen as the grandfather of many resource discovery metadata sets. This is only a subset of records management metadata and therefore it is simply insufficient.

Digital preservation

The main standard in this area is the Open Archival Information System (OAIS) reference model (ISO 14721:2003). It originates from the scientific data world (the National Aeronautics and Space Administration, NASA) but has been developed collaboratively by data archivists, librarians and archivists. The reference model offers a comprehensive overview of what is needed to preserve digital objects of any kind through time and technological changes, when they are no longer used within their original environment. In its essence the model has as its main functions:

- ingest
- storage
- access
- preservation planning
- data management
- administration.

The digital objects that have to be preserved should be submitted as submission information packages (SIPs), which will be transformed during ingest into archival information packages (AIPs) and can be made available through dissemination information packages (DIPs). Although it refers users only to migration as a preservation strategy, it is applicable to other strategies too. Since it is a reference model it has to be adapted to different contexts, such as archives and data centres, with different requirements. The model is accompanied by an information model and is widely accepted in scientific data centres, libraries and archives as a framework (ISO, 14721:2003) (OAIS, www.ccsds.org/documents/650x0b1.pdf).

OAIS is the focal point around which other standardization initiatives are being developed. An example is the attempt to devise a preservation metadata set by the Research Libraries Group (RLG) in collaboration with OCLC (www.rlg.org). Though the proposed set has not been formally established, it attracts a great deal of attention in the world of digital preservation. Other initiatives in this community are the so-called 'attributes of trusted digital repositories' and the PREMIS working group that has published in May 2005 guidelines for implementing metadata with respect to preservation.

Also, building upon OAIS is the coding and structure Metadata Encoding and Transmission Standard (METS: www.loc.gov/standards/mets/). This enables organizations to add descriptive, administrative and structural metadata to digital objects as textual and image-based works. It can be used for the different information packages in the OAIS model.

In relation to digital preservation initiatives to build file format registries are under way. Such registries describe existing file formats and could offer services for example that enable automatic transformation from one file format to another or that can check whether a file format is what it says it is. Currently, however, the development of those registries is still in its initial stage. Examples of registries are the UK National Archives' PRONOM (www.nationalarchives.gov.uk/pronom/), which actually contains descriptions but does not offer many services, and the DLF initiative to develop the Global Digital Format Registry (www.diglib.org/preserve.htm).

Use of models and methodologies

Having standards is nice, but it is even more important to be able to implement them and that may not be an easy task. The ISO 15489 standard provides organizations with a framework for records management. However, because of its rather abstract character it requires some interpretation and translation to make it applicable at the practical level. One of the methodologies helping this process is the Australian Design and Implementation of RecordKeeping Systems (DIRKS) methodology. An abstract of this methodology is included in the Technical Report accompanying the ISO 15489 standard (ISO, 15489-2:2001).

The DIRKS methodology consists of eight steps that help organizations, as stated on the website of the National Archives of Australia (www.naa.gov.au), to:

1 understand the business, regulatory and social context in which they operate (step A);
2 identify their need to create, control, retrieve and dispose of records (that is, their recordkeeping requirements) through an analysis of their business activities and environmental factors (steps B and C);

3 assess the extent to which existing organizational strategies (such as policies, procedures and practices) satisfy their recordkeeping requirements (step D);

4 redesign existing strategies or design new strategies to address unmet or poorly satisfied requirements (steps E and F); and

5 implement, maintain and review these strategies (steps G and H).

It is a very thorough approach, which has been used mainly in Australia. In Europe some organizations have picked it up but, perhaps not surprisingly, not many, if any, have used the whole process in detail.

This methodology shows not only what a challenge it is to implement proper records management, but also how broad it is. It cannot be addressed by one standard but should be a coherent system of policies, strategies, procedures, methods, processes and standards. To be successful it has to start from what is mentioned under the first bullet point – the business context.

In the previous paragraphs it has become clear that there is a bewildering array of standards and that is why there is the expression 'the nice thing about standards is that there are so many to choose from'. In practice, however, and despite the fact that we are creating huge amounts of information, its management, let alone the use of standards, often does not appear high on the priority list, if at all. In this respect the Information Management Capacity Check (IMCC; www.archives.ca/06/0603/060301_e.html), mainly developed in Canada, is a useful instrument and offers a good framework for changing information and records management. By identifying different levels of maturity, it allows organizations to assess the current situation based on a set of criteria, the possible risks and to set the short and medium term goals, all in close relationship with the business activities.

One aspect that should be included in this exercise is the relationship with possible other standards such as the standard on information security (ISO, 17799:2000) and the ISO 9000:2000 series on quality management systems. Information security can be viewed as an aspect of managing records in order to help guarantee authenticity, reliability and integrity, while records management in itself can be seen as an aspect of quality assurance. It is mentioned as such in the ISO 9000:2000 standard. Awareness of these standards therefore can help not only the positioning but also the strengthening of records management.

Standards in relation to audit and certification

The flipside of the use of standards is the need to be able to assess whether an organization complies with them or not. And that is where audit and certification come in. This special area is at the moment being rediscovered in the records management community. The stability of paper records and deeply rooted methods and procedures in the paper world have been shaken by the advent of digital objects and documents. The subsequent insecurity about how to manage those new objects together with their unstable and intangible nature, the transition many organizations are going through in order to adapt to the new digital world, and finally the recent financial scandals and the new legislation to prevent these, all contribute to the current popularity of audits and certification. An important aspect of auditing is whether organizations use and comply with standards. If they comply they can be certified.

It is therefore useful to be aware of standards in this specific area that auditors use to guide them in conducting audits: they include the Committee of Sponsoring Organisations of the Treadway Commission (COSO) framework (COSO, 1992); the Control Objectives for Information and Related Technology (COBIT) framework; and advice from ISACA (Information Systems Audit and Control Association), www.isaca.org; and IT Governance Institute (www.itgi.org/). COSO focuses on internal control and evaluating corporate governance, while COBIT supports especially the control of IT resources in relation to business requirements. As such both can also help in establishing a good framework for records and information management.

Further developments: dynamics

Although standards try to provide some stability in a dynamic environment they are themselves also subject to change. With growing experience, new insights as well as changing technology standards have to be adapted and updated. New versions will be published. Mostly these will be further refinements, which do not affect the basic principles. ISO 15489 was published in 2001, for example, and is under review at the moment.

New standards will emerge that build on existing ones or complement them. But with so many new standards emerging it can be difficult to choose what best suits a specific (business) context. It is therefore very important for any organization to identify and formulate the requirements for accomplishing its business activities before choosing any standard. Such an investment will often achieve a return because it will support more efficient working processes.

References

Bischoff, F. M., Hofman, H. and Ross, S. (eds) (2004) *Metadata in Digital Preservation: selected papers from an ERPANET seminar held in Marburg, 3–5 September 2003*, Marburg (Veröffentlichungen der Archivschule Marburg, nr. 40). See also www.erpanet.org/events/2003/marburg/index.php [accessed 1 September 2005].

Committee of Sponsoring Organisations of the National Commission of Fraudulent Financial Reporting (the Treadway Commission) (1992) *Internal Control – Integrated Framework*. Executive summary available at www.coso.org/publications/executive_summary_integrated_framework.htm. See also the report and presentations given at an ERPANET workshop in Antwerp, www.erpanet.org/events/2004/antwerpen/index.php [accessed 1 September 2005].

DLF initiative, www.diglib.org/preserve.htm [accessed 1 September 2005].

Dublin Core, http://dublincore.org/ [accessed 1 September 2005].

Information Management Capacity Check (IMCC) Tool and Methodology, www.archives.ca/06/0603/060301_e.html [accessed 1 September 2005].

InterPARES, www.interpares.org/ip2/ip2_description.cfm. The registry itself will become available on the project website. Another organization involved in metadata registries within the framework of interoperability of web services is OASIS, www.interpares.org/ip2/ip2_description.cfm [accessed 1 September 2005].

ISO 3166-1:1997, ISO 3166-2:1998 and ISO 3166-3:1999, *Codes for the Representation of Names of Countries and their Subdivisions*, Geneva, International Organization for Standardization.

ISO 8601:2000, *Data Elements and Interchange Formats – Information Interchange – Representation of Dates and Times*, Geneva, International Organization for Standardization.

ISO 9000 series:2000, *Quality Management Systems – Requirements*, Geneva, International Organization for Standardization.

ISO 17799:2000, *Information Technology – Guidelines for the Management of IT Security*, Geneva, International Organization for Standardization.

ISO 15489:2001, *Information and Documentation - Records Management Part 1: General, Part 2: Guidelines*, Geneva, International Organization for Standardization.

ISO 14721:2003, *Space Data and Information Transfer Systems – Open Archival Information System – Reference Model*, Geneva, International Organization for Standardization. The OAIS model can also be found on www.ccsds.org/documents/650x0b1.pdf [accessed 1 September 2005].

ISO/TS 23081-1:2004, *Information and Documentation - Records Management Processes - Metadata for Records – Part 1: Principles*; Parts 2 and 3 due for publication in 2005 and 2006; Geneva, International Organization for Standardization.

IT Governance Institute (www.itgi.org/) COBIT. See also the report and presentations given at an ERPANET workshop in Antwerp, www.erpanet.org/events/2004/ antwerpen/index.php [accessed 1 September 2005]

Metadata Encoding Transmission Standard (METS), www.loc.gov/standards/mets/ [accessed 1 September 2005].

Minnesota State Archives, www.mnhs.org/preserve/records/electronicrecords/ermetadata.html [accessed 1 September 2005].

MoReq: *Model Requirements for the Management of Electronic Records*, www.cornwell.co.uk/moreq [accessed 1 September 2005].

The National Archives, *Functional Requirements of Electronic Records Management Systems*, www.nationalarchives.gov.uk/electronicrecords/function.htm [accessed 1 September 2005].

The National Archives, *PRONOM: The File Format Registry*, www.nationalarchives.gov.uk/pronom/ [accessed 1 September 2005].

National Archives of Australia (1999) *Recordkeeping Metadata Standard for Commonwealth Agencies*, www.naa.gov.au/recordkeeping/control/rkms/summary.htm [accessed 1 September 2005]

National Archives of Australia (2001) *The DIRKS Manual*, www.naa.gov.au/recordkeeping/dirks/summary.html [accessed 1 September 2005].

Research Libraries Group, www.rlg.org [accessed 1 September 2005].

Standards Australia (1996) AS 4390:1-6, *Records Management*, Canberra, Standards Australia.

State Records New South Wales Australia, *Recordkeeping Metadata Standard*,
www.records.nsw.gov.au/publicsector/rk/rib/rib18.htm#NRKMS [accessed
1 September 2005].

Canadian Recordkeeping Metadata Forum,
www.collectionscanada.ca/metaforum/n11-232-e.html [accessed
1 September 2005].

The National Archives UK (2004) *Requirements for Electronic Records
Management systems, 2, Metadata Standard (e-GMS3)*,
www.govtalk.gov.uk/documents/Records_management_metadata_
standard_2002.doc [accessed 1 September 2005].

U.S. Department of Defense (2002) *Design Criteria Standard for Electronic
Records Management Software Applications*, DoD5015.2-STD, Washington,
US Department of Defense.

World Wide Web Consortium W3C, www.w3.org [accessed 1 September
2005].

Footnotes

1   Subcommittee SC11 is part of Technical Committee (TC) 46 *Information
and Documentation* and consists of 21 members and 11 observers.

2   The NARA website gives further explanation including why the standard
should be used. See
www.archives.gov/records_management/policy_and_guidance/bulletin_
2003_03.html [accessed 1 September 2005].

Chapter 3

Metadata matters

KATE CUMMING

Introduction

The word metadata is a difficult and obtuse one, but when the IT and the terminology are stripped away metadata in a records management context is essentially data that describes, contextualizes and facilitates the management of records. Good metadata enables good records management but, seen more broadly, the effective application of metadata can help the achievement of more extensive objectives, such as better information accessibility, maintenance of corporate memory and greater accountability in business operations.

Metadata is therefore a critical tool in any contemporary business environment. In the majority of business environments, however, metadata that contributes to records management objectives is either poorly implemented or not applied at all. To help determine how better to implement metadata in an organization, this chapter examines what metadata is in a records management context and focuses on a range of practical strategies to help guide metadata implementation.

Metadata in a records management context

Applied appropriately, the role of metadata in a records management context is to:

- identify records, the people or workgroups that create and use them and the areas of business they document
- establish connections between related records, between records and the people or workgroups that create and use them, between records and the business they document and between people and the business they perform
- help manage and preserve record content, structure and accessibility
- administer management requirements, including terms and conditions of access, use and disposal
- document actions performed upon records and their metadata
- facilitate the discovery, understanding and retrieval of records.

The application of metadata also enables a significant range of broader business objectives to be achieved. These include increased control, understanding, authenticity, security and accessibility of organizational information and the ability to reuse data as required. The ability to increase access and use of organizational information securely is an incredibly valuable commodity in today's business environment and is a key benefit that effective metadata implementation can facilitate.

There are many other types of metadata that differ in their scope and application from records management metadata. Prominent examples of metadata schema created by other communities to serve specific purposes include the Dublin Core standard, created to facilitate cross-domain information resource description (Dublin Core Metadata Initiative, 2004), and Standard Generalized Markup Language (SGML), a form of structural metadata used to break a document into its component parts to facilitate its mark-up and flexible, electronic representation.

Although there is a profusion of metadata standards within and beyond the records management community, it is important not to become too concerned about these, nor about the relationships and differences between them. Once the basic objectives of records management metadata strategies and the organization's requirements are understood, it becomes easier to differentiate between diverse standards and to choose a standard that is most appropriate to meet organizational needs. Alternatively, depending on the industry or organization sector, there may be one or several standards that need to be applied or a bespoke metadata schema may be developed based on specific organizational requirements. The organization needs to decide. The important thing is to understand what the metadata needs to do and then to apply it in the most effective way to help achieve the objectives.

In general, however, the value of records management metadata should not be underestimated. Records, as a form of accountable business information, are incredibly vulnerable in the electronic environment. Their structure, content, accessibility and meaning can be easily jeopardized and their ongoing physical existence is difficult to secure. The application of appropriate metadata can help to maintain records and preserve their structure, content, accessibility and meaning but, at a higher level, implementation of metadata can also help testify to the authenticity of records. The presumption of authenticity is critical in the electronic business environment. Because of their inherent vulnerabilities and the threats that they face, it is critical that records are able to be demonstrably valid and accountable chronicles of the business they document. Applying metadata can help testify to the authenticity of records by documenting their effective maintenance and management.

While acknowledging its value, however, it is important to identify that metadata is not the definitive solution to the recordkeeping dilemmas that confront us in the electronic environment. Metadata is certainly a tool that we can use when resolving these dilemmas but it must be remembered that metadata is only one component of accountable recordkeeping and business infrastructures. Metadata and the records to which it relates cannot exist in isolation. In the majority of business environments it is not appropriate to have records accompanied by a few cursory metadata elements. Instead records need to be managed in a controlled, coherent system and metadata needs to be applied as an integral component of this system.

A system in this context is not simply a software application designed to manage records or an application used to conduct business activities. As defined in *Strategies for Documenting Government Business: the DIRKS manual* (State Records Authority of New South Wales, 2003) a system is an organized collection of:

- people
- policies
- procedures

- tools (tools are recordkeeping instruments – disposal schedules, thesauri, access and security classification schemes, etc. – that are designed to help manage and control records through time)
- technology
- ongoing supporting education
- maintenance

which combine to ensure the efficient and accountable transaction of business. It is only if they are managed within systems that provide adequate support, structure and protection, that records will be regarded as useful and authoritative components of the organization's corporate knowledge.

In the electronic business environment metadata is becoming an increasingly significant component of these systems. As discussed above, this is because in many jurisdictions electronic records can only be regarded as authoritative and potentially as authentic if they are accompanied by metadata that identifies them and testifies to their appropriate management. It is therefore increasingly important that metadata is applied as a key component of accountable business infrastructures to describe records.

In many current implementations, however, metadata achieves few of these objectives. This is because much metadata is implemented in poorly designed, ad hoc systems that are not consistent with the definition of system outlined above and which have not been developed to meet business needs or to maximize the potential of metadata application. In addition, metadata is frequently not applied in all appropriate environments. In all organizations metadata should be applied in any environment where there is a requirement to create, maintain, produce and use accountable records of business operations. As a consequence, metadata that supports records management objectives should be applied in the majority of business systems in operation across organizations. Frequently, however, it is not. Designing and implementing metadata strategies is therefore about building better recordkeeping systems in organizations and achieving better organizational outcomes as a result.

Designing and implementing metadata strategies: the business context

So how can this be achieved? How can metadata be effectively applied within an appropriate infrastructure and used to facilitate the ongoing use and management of electronic records? The following discussion concerning the development and implementation of metadata strategies draws considerably from the strategy for designing and implementing recordkeeping systems (DIRKS Strategy), particularly the version of this strategy produced by the State Records Authority of New South Wales (2003) *Strategies for Documenting Government Business: the DIRKS manual*.

To summarize the recommended approach, to implement tailored metadata solutions for an organization effectively it is necessary to:

- know the staff and the organization's business needs and requirements
- know the existing business systems
- use the knowledge of business requirements and current business systems to develop tailored metadata solutions that remedy issues faced by the organization.

Know the staff and the organization's business needs and requirements

As with all business strategies, the first requirement when starting any type of metadata project is to commence the work with a thorough knowledge of the staff and its business. Knowing the staff involves understanding what colleagues do and how their work is undertaken. A good grasp of the organization's business needs, its corporate environment and the legal, business and community requirements it faces is needed. This knowledge, while broad, will serve to ground the approach to metadata development making the strategy devised immediately relevant and useful to the organization.

The issue of legal, business and community requirements is particularly important. These requirements are key drivers and regulators of an organization's business operations. It is therefore important to have a good understanding of the requirements that affect the areas of business being examined. Compiling a list of the requirements affecting the organization as a whole, or that affect each specific business unit, will provide a means of developing a comprehensive metadata strategy for the organization. It will identify how and where metadata should be applied to help meet the specific business needs.

Example 3.1   Considering how metadata can be applied
to meet business requirements

A section's operating instructions may say that the 'name of complainant
must be captured with every complaint received'. By ensuring that a
specific piece of metadata, the name of the complainant, can be captured
with every record of a complaint, metadata is being used to satisfy this
requirement.

Other requirements will be partially satisfied through the use of metadata.
For example, the requirement that 'licence applications must be retained
for 50 years' is unlikely to be completely satisfied by metadata implementation. However, in an appropriately designed business system, metadata
can be used to facilitate the management, migration and appropriate
disposal of records. Thus, in this instance, metadata is a tool that can help
to ensure that records are retained for as long as is specified by the
business requirements.

[Based on an example provided in *Strategies for Documenting Government
Business: the DIRKS manual* (State Records Authority of New South
Wales, 2003)]

Know the existing business systems

Once there is a good idea of business needs an understanding of how
business is currently conducted is then necessary. This requires a good
knowledge of what systems are used to transact business, how they perform
their operations and what technology they use. The metadata that they
currently capture must be identified and an understanding of the business
rules that are in place to regulate activity in the system gained. This will help
to determine whether the current metadata capture is adequate.

Example 3.2   Assessing systems to determine if they
meet business requirements

One organization with responsibility for licensing was subject to a legal
requirement which stated that 'Licensees should not be given access to
the records of other licensees'. To determine whether the system they use
for managing their licensing records was able to meet this specific
requirement, people assessing the system asked:

Continued on next page

Example 3.2   *Continued*

- Is the system capable of restricting access to designated users? That is, is adequate metadata in place within the system to ensure that only authorized users can access records?
- Does system user training make it clear that access restrictions apply to licensee records?
- Do the policies that are part of this system inform staff of these access rules?

If the system complies with each of these requirements, it is likely that the organization is meeting its legal requirement to restrict access to license records.

The example demonstrates that there is a symbiotic relationship between all aspects of a business system, in this case the metadata within a system and the business rules and training support that sustain the system use. Therefore metadata cannot be examined in isolation. Metadata is an integral part of the records infrastructure but all components of a system need to be examined, including business rules, staff behaviour and system user training guidelines, to ensure all are operating consistently and in line with organizational objectives. It is only when all these elements are working harmoniously that it is possible to ensure the business requirements are being met.

[Based on an example provided in *Strategies for Documenting Government Business: the DIRKS manual* (State Records Authority of New South Wales, 2003)]

Example 3.3   Problems identified during a system
                              assessment

An organization operates a business system. Significant fraud starts occurring within the organization. An investigation is commenced and the following flaws in the system are identified:

- There is an absence of full audit trails – incomplete metadata is captured about the actions performed upon records in the system, particularly the specific staff member making changes and the rationale for the changes.
- Infrequent checks are made to ensure that staff access levels are appropriate.

Continued on next page

Example 3.3   *Continued*

- There are too many staff with access to 'modify/create' records.
- There is ongoing failure to check for and remove 'modify/create' access following staff resignation or when staff move to different sections of the organization.
- There is ongoing failure to automatically remove 'modify/create' access when temporary employment ceases.
- Exception reports, which alert administrators to system breaches, are not being generated or used adequately.

In this scenario the problems are twofold. There are issues with the metadata within the system. Adequate information about the management of records is not being maintained. The system does not have the capacity to record all the data necessary to help preserve the records' accountability. The gaps in the system's metadata capacities mean that record integrity cannot be assured and this ultimately leads to the conduct of fraud. In the electronic environment, good and accountable metadata is critical to the presumption of authenticity over the records to which it relates. Be sure then to protect the metadata as it is vital in protecting a significant proportion of the corporate information.

Secondly, there are gaps in the organization's policy framework. When implementing a metadata strategy, it is important to ensure that rules are in place to support that strategy. It is also important that these rules are adhered to over time. An excellent strategy might have been developed but it can be derailed in implementation if adequate and ongoing care is not maintained. Therefore it is necessary to ensure that only relevant staff have the capacity to access records and their metadata. The definition of 'relevant' staff needs to be regularly reviewed and staff regularly reminded of their responsibilities. Remember that metadata is only one component of organizational systems and all components need to be working consistently for an adequate recordkeeping infrastructure to be in place.

[Based on an example provided in *Strategies for Documenting Government Business: the DIRKS manual* (State Records Authority of New South Wales, 2003)]

The metadata captured within a system can be identified by examining the system itself, by reading system documentation and by assessing data dictionaries and data models. Staff will also be able to describe the data they create and manage in their daily business operations.

Another way to test the capacities of business systems and to identify the metadata they contain is to use existing metadata standards. Choose a range of standards that specify records management requirements. Others that pertain to the specific area of business being assessed may also be selected. These benchmarks can be used to test whether the business system being assessed captures all relevant metadata deemed appropriate by the best practice standards. If it does not, the metadata standards can be used as models to guide improved metadata implementation in the business systems.

Develop tailored metadata solutions that remedy issues faced by the organization

Specific system assessments will give an understanding of any problems that currently exist in the organization's business operations and will help in understanding how improved metadata implementation and maintenance can aid meeting legal and business requirements. Once there is this understanding, a metadata strategy that can help to remedy the issues identified can begin to be developed. A metadata strategy is simply a range of ideas about how metadata can be used to meet the business requirements. A metadata strategy could be something as simple as improved user training to make sure that staff are capturing all necessary information, or the development of a new database with improved metadata capacities to completely revise how work in a particular business area is undertaken. The extent of the strategy will be dependent on the range of business needs identified during the system assessments.

Designing and implementing metadata strategies: metadata issues

At the point of developing a metadata strategy there are a number of issues to be considered. When developing a strategy it is essential to:

- incorporate records management functionality
- identify where metadata is going to come from
- determine where the metadata is to be stored
- develop authoritative rules, policies or guidelines to govern metadata attribution

- consider how metadata can further contribute to record usability and understanding.

Incorporate records management functionality

As discussed, records management functionality is necessary to ensure the ongoing usability, manageability and trustworthiness of the organization's records. Yet it is frequently left out of the system design or system redesign process. Be sure to consider issues such as records disposal. Can metadata be built into the system that identifies how long the different classes of records contained in the system need to be maintained? Can business rules be set across a database that specify retention requirements? Can metadata be used to prescribe rules that will ensure the organizational operations are consistent with freedom of information, privacy requirements, commercial-in-confidence and other access-related issues that may need to be considered? Ensure that any implementation of records management metadata is supported by staff education programmes and the development of user manuals. These tools will enable staff to apply records management metadata appropriately, in accordance with any legal requirements.

Identify where metadata is going to come from

For any solution implemented, one constant requirement will be to identify where the metadata is going to come from. Metadata can be generated in a number of ways. For example, it can be:

- input by staff
- automatically captured by the system when conducting business transactions
- automatically created by system according to rules established within it (such as sequential file numbering, automatic attribution of disposal class according to classified title applied to file and so on)
- drawn from recordkeeping tools such as disposal authorities, thesauri and so on
- derived from the security classification scheme(s) employed within the organization
- obtained from IT system controls, inherited from logins and so on
- inherited from the dates and times presented by system clocks.

Where financially and technically feasible it is useful to consider automatic capture of metadata and to build as much interoperability as possible between systems in order to facilitate metadata inheritance. Consider where metadata can be automatically derived from and assess the possibility of data exchange between systems. Look at the business environment surrounding the system, the recordkeeping tools developed and the data that is maintained in other systems. Try to see where data can be automatically extracted or derived from, to save users from having to enter significant amounts of information and to help ensure better data consistency.

Understanding metadata as an active entity will also help to implement the dynamic functionality it can enable in the business and records management operations. For example, if a technical solution to the business needs is being developed ask whether the metadata being implemented enables the automatic trigger of record disposal operations. Can the metadata and system be configured to enable records to be automatically dispatched along a workflow? Remember that implementing recordkeeping metadata should not be about creating data profiles but about facilitating process. In contemporary systems, much metadata is implemented as a descriptive profile, which passively describes a record. If metadata is applied more actively and within systems that can use the data to trigger a business process and automate activity, it becomes a much more powerful and useful tool. Consider how this can be achieved in the organization.

Determine where the metadata is to be stored

Metadata can be stored in business systems, records management applications, databases, distributed systems and even in paper form. Consider the option or combination of options that work best with the needs and the existing technologies. In making decisions about metadata storage, it is important to remember the need to make active use of the metadata – does the storage option chosen enable this? It is also vital that if a distributed management option is chosen for the metadata – that is if records and the metadata that describes them are stored in different applications – persistent links are able to be reliably maintained between them. Whatever storage option is chosen, ensure that the metadata is meaningful, well maintained and able to meet the organizational requirements.

Develop authoritative rules, policies or guidelines to govern metadata attribution

When developing ways to apply metadata to meet the records management needs, the work will be easier and organizational recordkeeping more efficient and accountable if authoritative rules, policies or guidelines are used to govern metadata attribution. Recordkeeping tools such as disposal authorities, access and security classification schemes and classification schemes should be the types of authoritative sources used to derive metadata values. Controlled vocabularies or prescribed metadata values may be used in other parts of the system. Use of such values can make metadata application easier for staff and will allow standardized and consistent metadata values to be applied. Remember that whatever tools and schemes are employed to provide metadata values, staff will need to be trained in their use to ensure that they are able to apply the correct metadata from the relevant scheme.

Consider how metadata can further contribute to record usability and understanding

Finally, when designing strategies for better metadata implementation it is also important to remember the valuable role that metadata plays in record usability and understanding. When examining the systems and determining ways in which metadata can improve their performance, consider whether additional metadata could facilitate information searching and retrieval. Significant amounts of staff time are lost searching for corporate information. Consider how the application of better descriptive data could help remedy this issue.

General tips for metadata implementation

When developing solutions that will enable the business requirements to be met, there are a number of key rules about metadata that need to be remembered. These are:

- Metadata application should be scalable.
- Metadata solutions should be developed using consultation and liaison.
- Metadata will continue to accrue and evolve.
- Metadata must be managed.

- Metadata may need to be maintained for longer than the record to which it relates.

Metadata application should be scalable

Remember that with metadata it is rarely one size fits all, as a range of different metadata strategies may be required to meet the disparate needs of the business environment. For example, in one business area that operates in a high-risk environment it may be decided that the technological components of a business system need to be redesigned to enable more metadata capture and to potentially automate much of this capture.

In another business area where the technical infrastructure is adequate but metadata capture is poor, the decision may be to work more closely with staff to help explain how better metadata capture can help them in their day-to-day operations and to identify ways in which they can capture and maintain this metadata. Different strategies may therefore be appropriate in different areas of the organization. Consider the disparate needs of the business areas and the variety of staff. Metadata is a flexible tool. Be sure to implement it in a flexible manner.

Remember too that metadata can exist at different levels of aggregation and can be used to describe different types of things. For example, metadata may be captured to describe:

- individual records (such as a title or unique identifier for an individual record)
- groups of records (such as disposal rules applied at the file level)
- systems (such as access rules applied to a whole personnel records database).

The levels and types of metadata that will work best to meet the recordkeeping requirements need to be determined. Metadata is a scalable and flexible tool so use it in ways that best meet the particular objectives.

Metadata solutions should be developed using consultation and liaison

Do not feel decisions about metadata implementation have to be made alone. Talk to people across the business areas being examined. Staff will know the types of information that will facilitate their jobs or enable them to access information better. Use their feedback to help identify the metadata that should be captured to support a range of business activities. Use the expertise of those familiar with the areas of business under operation, but do not doubt personal knowledge. Contribute personal ideas based on the research conducted and discuss different options with the staff involved.

Effective implementation of metadata will also be contingent on liaison with data and IT managers, systems analysts and other business management staff, all of whom will combine with records managers to identify the ways, means and business benefits of metadata implementation.

Metadata will continue to accrue and evolve

In the design and implementation process it is important to remember that the metadata the organization creates will need to evolve through time. When it is created, a record will be described as it exists at the point of its creation. Elements of this description, such as the date and time of the record's creation, will remain constant through the record's lifespan. However much of the description will need to be updated as the record itself changes. For example, the record will be subject to different management processes. Its physical structure may change as it is migrated through a range of systems. Different people may use and even add to it over time. It will become connected to an increasing number of other records.

All original metadata description will need to be preserved, but new descriptive details arising from the range of processes and transformations the record has undergone will need to accrue. Consequently metadata needs to evolve to ensure it continues to reflect the reality and requirements of the record. Be aware of this when designing metadata systems or when liaising with software vendors or IT staff over system design. Be sure the systems have the capacity to manage and maintain this ongoing evolution and accrual.

Metadata must be managed

Like any other valuable business commodity metadata itself requires management. It will need to be monitored to ensure that it continues to reference appropriate information. Staff will need to be regularly kept informed of their responsibilities in relation to its creation and management. In electronic systems, the ongoing accessibility of metadata will have to be monitored. Staff with responsibility for system migration and conversion will need to be aware of the need to maintain metadata through system change. It is also crucial that the connections between metadata and the records to which it relates are maintained through time and system change. Metadata management should therefore be referenced in all organizational data and system management requirements.

Metadata may need to be maintained for longer than the record to which it relates

Be aware that there may be legal and/or organizational requirements to maintain metadata beyond the lifespan of the record to which it relates. For example, a record may have been destroyed in accordance with an authorized disposal authority but the organization may need to maintain the metadata that identifies what the record documented, the dates of its existence, the uses to which it was subject and the authorizations that allowed its destruction. It is important to consider such requirements during system design and to ensure that IT staff, or those with responsibility for system development and maintenance, are aware of such requirements and build in system capacities to accommodate them.

Conclusion

In today's fast-paced electronic world, records managers and others involved in information management may feel that they are losing confidence in their ability to actually manage records. Multiple technologies, vendors and systems seem to exist and records themselves appear to be evolving into ever more varied forms. Metadata, however, should be seen as a key tool that can assist in the effective and accountable management of electronic records and the more efficient management and use of organizational information. Metadata strategies have their basis in traditional records management and archival practices but today should be regarded as key components of business administration and vital elements of multipurpose organizational information management frameworks.

Metadata is a key business instrument but its implementation needs to be a considered exercise. Metadata is not a standalone tool. It needs to be implemented in appropriate systems that provide adequately for the business needs. Metadata is only one component of business systems but it is a key component of these systems and significant value in a wide variety of areas can come from its deployment.

References

Dublin Core Metadata Initiative (2004) *Dublin Core Metadata Element Set, Version 1.1, Element Description*, www.dublincore.org/documents/dces/ [accessed 1 September 2005].

ISO 15489-1:2001, *Information and Documentation – Records Management – Part 1: General*, Geneva, International Organization for Standardization.

ISO 15489-2:2001, *Information and Documentation – Records Management – Part 2: Guidelines*, Geneva, International Organization for Standardization.

ISO 23081-1:2004, *Information and Documentation – Records Management Processes – Metadata for Records – Part 1: Principles*, Geneva, International Organization for Standardization.

McKemmish, S., Acland, G., Ward, N. and Reed, B. (1999) Describing Records in Context in the Continuum: the Australian Recordkeeping Metadata Schema, www.sims.monash.edu.au/research/rcrg/publications/archiv01.htm [accessed 1 September 2005].

State Records Authority of New South Wales (June 2003) *Strategies for Documenting Government Business: the DIRKS manual*, www.records.nsw.gov.au/publicsector/DIRKS/final/title.htm [accessed 1 September 2005].

Chapter 4

Digital preservation – 'the beautiful promise'[1]

DAVID RYAN

Introduction

How will our grandchildren judge us? Will they remember us as conscientious custodians, who adapted quickly to the needs of the electronic information age, or will they smile forgivingly at museum stores and library shelves filled with mute magnetic media, their contents long past any chance of retrieval? Digital preservation in 2005 stands at a crossroads. Will archivists and librarians forgo the comfort of digitizing their existing holdings and turn instead to the complex but more promising task of saving the 'new history', being born digital all around us – seemingly ephemeral but glorious in its potential?

Beginning with an archival fundamental among the seeming anarchy of the information age, there will soon come a time when users stop hitting the print button as a reflex action and storage is only measured in bytes. At this point, will 'permanent' retention be replaced by short-term, technology-dependent retention? Who is brave enough to even discuss this question with colleagues? Who is measuring this substitution effect – the eventual demise of 'new' paper records and their *complete* replacement by the electronic? And who is making plans to deal with this effectively?

This chapter does not present a detailed technical discussion about methods of digital preservation. These methods are not universally agreed and will need to be subjected to further empirical investigation over the next few years. Instead, the chapter offers a consideration of the purposes and context of digital preservation, followed by some practical advice on setting up a digital preservation business unit within or for an organization that requires such a function. In addition to historical records or library services' requirements for digital preservation, this advice will also be of use to businesses managing their current records, whether governmental or in the corporate sector. Major changes in legislation with implications for records management, such as Sarbanes-Oxley in the USA (US Congress, 2002) and freedom of information legislation in the UK, mean that managing electronic records across major operating system and utility applications lifecycles has become a necessity for many businesses.

The word 'record' is used throughout to denote an electronic object(s); any discussion of intellectual property ownership issues or focus on any particular type of record, whether administrative or published, is largely avoided.

The records

To set the context for any strategies for digital preservation it is important to understand the challenges that lie at the heart of the problem.

Authoring software is not stable over time. This can be as short as days, as computers are updated with full releases or service packs automatically through web services. As these changes are not documented fully in the public domain and companies make no promises to support records *unchanged* when viewed later, so we cannot rely on software at present to preserve the record.

Instead, at least for the foreseeable future, it will be necessary to take an approach based on understanding the users' preferred methods of access, which is the primary reason for preservation. Readers will expect records to be delivered to them – what they can access from their browser, including, perhaps, audio versions of text for blind readers and versions delivered to mobile users. It can be assumed that they do not expect to have to come physically to 'read' electronic records in the reading rooms.

This may not be as problematic as it might appear. If we start at today's desktop, with broadband internet access, and work backwards, by far the greatest volume of records has been produced in the last 15 years, and the vast majority of these records have been created using Microsoft applications or were designed for web presentation.

Using a historical timeframe, from 1965 to 1985 mainframe systems can be considered as legacy systems. The great success of dataset preservation services has been based on the migration to standard format. Web-based presentation of such records and a variety of downloadable formats have not proved insurmountable, in most instances, as the records have simple structures and behaviours.

Over time, electronic records may require a new form of preservation. In ideal conditions, existing physical originals suffer slow, mostly imperceptible, entropy over hundreds of years. With digital records within much shorter timescales an '*authenticity continuum*' [2] will probably need to be addressed.

The advantage of the concept of an authenticity continuum (Figure 4.1) is that it allows the justification of actions at policy level for records of a particular type, with supporting technical documentation explaining predicates and variations.

This policy level justification will enable pricing models to be produced for migration decisions. It may well be that the cost of developing migration techniques needs to be shared across institutions to make them affordable. This already happens for physical preservation and conservation.

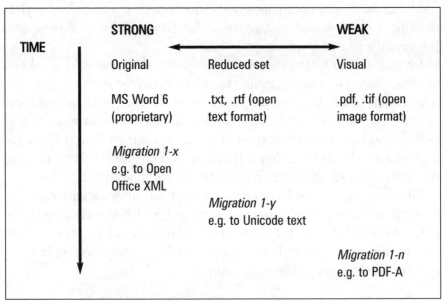

Figure 4.1   The authenticity continuum

Over time, will there be levels of authenticity? A true record versus a convenient information presentation – should we differentiate? The trustworthiness of migrations and the management systems of the organization as a whole are key. ISO 17799:2000 is already established as a standard measure in this field. This subject is being explored further in the Research Libraries Group Digital Repository Certification Task Force (www.rlg.org).

The fundamental problem will be at what point does a record lose validity? This will be complicated as always in questions of preservation, in that different users of the records are looking for different things and therefore have different views on authenticity. This will be further explored in sections on legal issues and access, below, but it might be useful to consider the information management model shown in Figure 4.2 (BSI, PD 0010, 1997) in the task.

This model should allow the identification of 'sudden step' degradation and discontinuities in the preservation of records. It would allow us to understand the degree of degradation of transformation and state, with general agreement, the minimum resolution required.

When we are taking action, this action will show clear value. Other issues, such as the currency of use of data or repackaging of elements for novel uses, unforeseen and quite different from those they were created for,

---

1   Classification of data
2   Duty of care
3   Business processes and procedures
     a. Documentation
4   Enabling technologies
     a. Existing
     b. Developing
        i. Own
        ii. By others (e.g. other projects, international standards work)
5   Audit
     a. Business (Business Plan targets, internal audit reviews – financial models and operational logic)
     b. Technical (project management and technical models, international standards)
     c. Customers/stakeholders' views

Figure 4.2   Five steps to good information management

could be accounted for in the pricing model and used, where appropriate, to offset some of the expense of the preservation work. This last statement, however, does beg the question of how much of what future users will expect can be guessed.

Strategies

The digital preservation function needs to be linked to the strategic business aims of the organization and, as a new idea, will require a strong business case and key senior champions in order to attract funding from existing competing demands. To ensure they are effective, consider putting a new organizational structure in place first, then move on to recruitment. It is best to avoid being forced to take surplus staff from within the organization. Technical competence and personal enthusiasm for the demanding work are paramount. The new organizational structure will give these new recruits a sense of worth and will inform the existing departments that the organization is committed to the new task ahead. Furthermore, according to Beagrie and Jones (www.dpconline.org/graphics/handbook/), strategies centred on an understanding of where the record is in its lifecycle, an analysis of what needs to be preserved, why and for how long 'will form a core component of corporate policy development to address digital preservation'.

Collecting and managing

How many of us have made a list of major recent events or business projects relevant to our organization? What was printed out? What was created on magnetic media? What was transferred to new media? What was destroyed/left on original media? Do any of us have a positive answer to even one of these questions? A collections plan, linked to overall organizationally relevant themes, will be needed. This will allow curators of electronic records not only to be confident that key topics are covered, but also how many objects are held and what technical dependencies these records have. Accurate information on volume and variety can then be used for assessing preservation costs and workload.

People

People are the most important resource in digital preservation and must be acquired first. It is important to understand in what order to recruit people. The most senior posts may not be the first recruited, as recruitment should reflect the business plans put in place to support the strategic aims. It may well be that in the longer term, digital preservation takes over functions previously the responsibility of other departments, for greater operational efficiency or digital preservation staff move to other departments to *e-enable* their business processes. At all times, good communications with existing functions must be maintained, whether they are formally named as stakeholders in the communications plan (see below) or not.

Consider also that as the department grows further application-type specific archivists will be required. This can be compared to conservation staff specializing on such traditional formats as book-binding or paper repair.

An example of an internal organization structure for a digital preservation function is provided in Figure 4.3.

The skills required for digital preservation will need to be defined carefully. The UK National Archives set up a digital preservation department between 2001 and 2004 consisting of 12 staff. Digital preservation job adverts were presented on The National Archives' website as helping to build a service integral to its overall business aims, even where the candidate requirements were a departure from those normally seen in a heritage organization. The BBC Information and Archives department has 'media managers' – these staff help manage material from its creation, through its production lifecycle and into the archive according to the BBC's Media Management Policy.

Technical roles are likely to be found in candidates with an engineering background and commonly, extensive experience of large-scale systems management in data centres. Information managers who have extensive IT knowledge will be needed to frame the business requirements. It may be prudent to recruit a communications officer solely for the digital preservation function. Explaining what the unit is doing to meet stakeholder needs and how it relates to the existing departments will need careful exposition. More generally, graduate level qualifications in library, archival or computing-related subjects, and an interest in digital preservation, will be essential. Some previous experience in collection management, and involvement in large-scale projects would be an advantage.

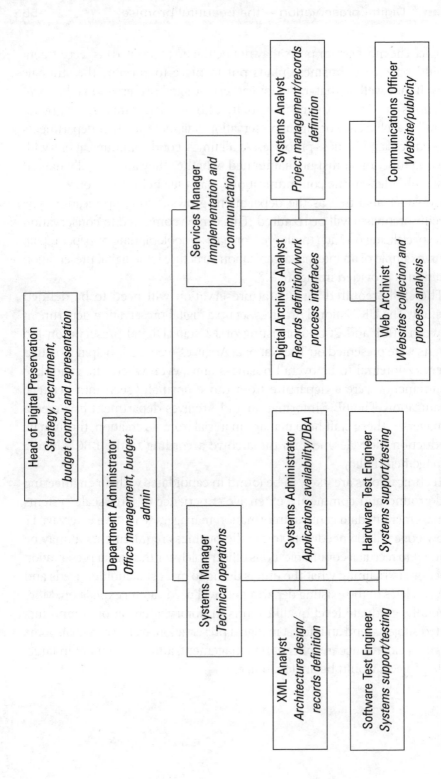

Figure 4.3 Example of a digital preservation department organization chart

Communication

The new function may want to produce a communications strategy. This can be done either within the unit itself, by a consultant or with input from colleagues in the press office or marketing department. A plan will be required, as digital preservation will be a new topic whose importance needs explaining to colleagues and stakeholders alike. Moreover, good communications help defeat any internal resistance. When budget and headcount may be getting diverted to a new function, those losing budgets may not always be far-sighted.

Measuring the success of communications is not difficult in itself, and press and marketing colleagues will have established methods for all kinds of interactions with the media and the public, whether in print, on screen or in person.

The communications plan should reflect the key business targets and be reviewed and updated at regular intervals, for example, yearly. The plan should be overhauled once the digital preservation function is firmly established.

Systems

The programs and hardware that manage the digital objects will themselves become obsolete. The key issue is to ensure the *authenticity* of the records themselves. All systems should be focused on this end, and should employ commercial off-the-shelf (COTS) products and well established data centre processes wherever possible for reliable operations. As the primary purpose of digital preservation is to avoid the loss of *any* record, a regime of 'chronic' maintenance of hardware and software with multiple redundancy of the records is essential. All disaster recovery plans should be hot-tested at regular intervals, and budget will need to be set aside to ensure that these exercises can be carried out.

ICT staff will be responsible for corporate IT operations such as server and network availability and software procurement. Formal service level agreements can be introduced to avoid resource conflicts.

Through outsourcing and consortia, some organizations have developed a business model that will allow a mature IT contracting market to supply services and products for digital preservation using and extending existing products and make the development of new applications or equipment economically credible. This has happened, for example, with the UK Web

Archiving Consortium (www.webarchive.org.uk). The consortium approach allows for the development of new products and services by spreading the burden of costs across a number of years, and allowing varied contributions from interested parties. Outsourcing allows an organization to take advantage of existing services or products to achieve savings from economies of scale or acquire specialist skills from suppliers.

Procedures

Procedures will be needed throughout the organization to ensure that electronic records are appropriately created, captured, organized and retained. For the digital preservation function itself this will mean technical procedures, training documentation and system administration guides for all operations. Procedures will also be required for administrative tasks, such as induction and out-of-hours contact.

All procedures should be technically accurate and as brief as possible. A management system for the production, editing, review and updating of all procedures should be put in place with a member of staff made responsible for its administration. This duty should be reflected in the relevant job description.

Research and development

As digital preservation is a developing area of information work, an extensive research agenda will be useful. This can be based on the work of others, as there is much development and exploration work carried out in computing, both practical and theoretical. Journals, books and websites exist in plenty as sources of reference. It may be necessary to implement a management system for managing the research library. Consider downloading information from the web into the system, where allowed, as sites can disappear.

All actions carried out on the records should be tested in a computer laboratory environment first, if possible. This will enable their efficacy to be proven and a detailed record kept when the actions are carried out for real. The program to test records before they are loaded into any storage system will need to make sure:

- they work programmatically
- the contents have not been corrupted prior to transfer
- they do not contain unnecessary files.

The National Archives has detailed its research programme on its website (www.nationalarchives.gov.uk/preservation/research/digital.htm). The National Library of Australia's PADI website (www.nla.gov.au/padi) has a section listing current and recently completed projects, and the Dspace (www.dspace.org) and VDC (www.thedata.org) sites are examples of communities of research, systems development and service delivery.

Legal issues

Doron Swade (2001) has commented that what will support digital preservation most effectively is 'legislation to the desktop' – what the user has available will define what can be done. He went on to comment that it would be necessary to break down the process of how digital records are created and understand their management as well as the management of paper objects is understood. The key is that records must suffer 'no penalty to the passage of time'.

The Testbed Digitale Bewaring project (www.digitaleduurzaamheid.nl/home.cfm) in the Netherlands and various web archiving projects have considered the societal and legal context of digital preservation – what society regards as a record and what society regards as authentic in the electronic domain. In a report to UNESCO and the International Council on Archives (www.ica.org/biblio/Study13_2Erev.pdf), Laura Miller (2004) highlighted the challenges to authenticity of electronic records as including 'the weakness of existing legislative, organisational, and policy frameworks for the management of electronic records'.

Can we take the view that what users believe is authentic *is* authentic and that societal assumptions of what has meaning will result in agreement on the realistic boundaries of evidential proof? In the USA, the Spinelli Corporation publishes (www.spinellicorp.com/cfnewsletter/) an archive of computer forensics and electronic discovery case law summaries. *The Good Practice Guide for Computer-based Electronic Evidence*, produced by the Association of Chief Police Officers (ACPO, 2003) in the UK, was updated as recently as 2003.

Access

In April 2005, the BBC announced the launch of the Creative Archive Licence (http://creativearchive.bbc.co.uk). The language used on the BBC website to describe how 'you can rip, mix and share the BBC' clearly

indicates an experience that is far from what public archive users would
have expected only a decade ago. The end goal is increasingly online
access by colleagues, customers or the public. It is important for digital
preservation to work closely with ICT, reader services and marketing to:

*   understand the users
*   understand their goals
*   understand the context of use
*   understand the essentials of product satisfaction.

Electronic records support 'information packaging' to answer structured
questions or presentation aggregations through automated analysis and
selection across distributed record sets. It will be important not to lose sight
of the original record when information products can be created so easily.

Over the last 20 years users have become familiar with and more skilled
at accessing the information they want and this will continue apace. The
result will be that the 'deep' subject and classification skills that information
professionals have will become ever more important. The manual preparation
of catalogues, even where the catalogues themselves are electronic, is
being replaced with automatic index generation. Google,[3] and the art of
relevance ranking, has now taken its place as a core tool for researchers.
Search technologies are deployed 'on the fly' – users store saved searches
to reuse and websites offer personalization based on previous search
terms, pages clicked and objects selected within those pages.

Understanding what different services different types of users want will
become a critical success factor. With constrained public sector budgets,
and the development of the 'information economy', working with third party
firms to provide value added services and products may well continue to
expand.

Looking to the future

The information world of the future will be about the management of digital
assets and digital preservation is a function of this. Work has progressed on
standards driven formats for electronic records, mainly based on XML. This
has been painfully slow, and there is still almost no international agreement
on subject-based internal structures for records as opposed to catalogue
descriptions (www.loc.gov/z3950/agency/profiles/collections.html). This

is a reflection of the fact that the focus for most users of information in records is immediate ready access not long-term meaning. Being optimistic, however, one could expect the need for standardized exchange of data (especially when solely machine to machine) to become more widespread as electronic records become all pervasive in mainstream business operations.

Work has begun on a wide range of associated topics, and this is reflected in resources like the PADI website. For example, the work of Bennett, Hendley, Sanett, Weinberger and others on cost modelling (www.nla.gov.au/padi/topics/5.html), which PADI brings together, is compelling. To have *determined* management of electronic records requires an understanding of what the benefits are compared with the costs over an extended period of time. That this is not well understood, and certainly not applied, despite the recent well-reported examples of poor management of electronic records, is worrying after more than half a century of computer use. If this is not addressed, then my optimism will be misplaced.

Returning to my opening comments on a crossroads reached, which path will information professionals take? Let's hope they take the road less travelled, at least so far. This road may be hard and bumpy, but at least it does not peter out at the gates of a closed-down paper mill.

References

Association of Chief Police Officers (2003) *Good Practice Guide for Computer-based Electronic Evidence*, London, NHTCU (National Hi-Tec Crime Unit).

BBC Creative Archive, http://creativearchive.bbc.co.uk [accessed 1 September 2005].

Beagrie, N. and Jones, M., www.dpconline.org/graphics/handbook/ [accessed 1 September 2005]. Includes a discussion of the records lifecycle and how digital preservation is affected by different institutional needs.

BSI, PD 0010 (1997) *The Principles of Good Practice for Information Management*, British Standards Institution, www.bsi-global.com/ICT/KM/pd0010.xalter [accessed 1 September 2005].

Dspace, www.dspace.org/ [accessed 1 September 2005].

ISO 17799:2000 *Information Technology: code of practice for information security management*, Geneva, International Organization for Standardization.

Miller, L. (2004) *Authenticity of Electronic Records. A report prepared for UNESCO and the International Council on Archives* (ICA Study 13-2), Paris, ICA, www.ica.org/biblio/Study3_2Erev.pdf.

The National Archives, www.nationalarchives.gov.uk/preservation [accessed 1 September 2005].

The National Archives Digital Research Programme, www.nationalarchives.gov.uk/preservation/research/digital.htm [accessed 1 September 2005].

National Library of Australia, PADI website, www.nla.gov.au/padi/ [accessed 1 September 2005].

Research Libraries Group Digital Repository Certification Task Force, www.rlg.org [accessed 1 September 2005].

Swade, D. (2001) Presentation at a meeting at the National Museum of Science and Industry, London, 23 November.

Testbed Digitale Bewaring project, www.digitaleduursaamheid.nl/home.cfm [accessed 1 September 2005].

US Congress (2002) Public Company Accounting Reform and Investor Protection Act (commonly referred to as the Sarbanes-Oxley Act), http://news.findlaw.com/hdocs/docs/gwbush/sarbanesoxley072302.but.

UK Web Archiving Consortium, www.webarchive.org.uk/ [accessed 1 September 2005].

Virtual Data Center, www.thedata.org/ [accessed 1 September 2005].

Footnotes

1   Dr Doron Swade, formerly Assistant Director and Head of Collections at the National Museum of Science and Industry, London at 'Practical Experiences in Digital Preservation', The National Archives, Kew, 2–4 April 2003; www.nationalarchives.gov.uk/preservation/news/conference/media/06swade.wma.

2   Informal discussion with Dr David Thomas and colleagues, The National Archives, UK, 2003.

3   This chapter was prepared using Microsoft Word 97 – the word Google is underlined in red as I type – it does not exist in the Word dictionary.

Chapter 5

Research in electronic records management

XIAOMI AN

Introduction

By extending the range of usable knowledge and by applying analysis and theory to real problems, research also extends our ability to illuminate further problems and to generate solutions to them.

Information technology has a widening range of applications in organizations and in society. This has presented records managers with challenges and opportunities. To meet the challenges and to exploit the opportunities, research projects have played an increasingly important part in developing the discipline in the electronic and digital environment. As Hedstrom (2004) pointed out, unprecedented changes caused by new information technologies have changed the application of archival theory, and there are many new areas of professional practice that still lack a useful theoretical basis or standards of practice. Research into a wide range of issues must precede the development of a useful knowledge base for contemporary archival problems. Research is a necessary bridge between theory and practice, and it can supply consistently credible and useful tools for records managers (Pemberton, 1992, 46). What progress has been made in research and by research in electronic records management? What can we learn from current research projects? What are the future directions for research in electronic records management?

A review of the literature shows a great number of recent articles on electronic records management, but among these only a few deal with the

metadata model, applied once in a specific environment, can then be used many times to meet a range of business purposes (Upward, 1996, 1997, 2000; Evans, McKemmish and Bhoday, 2004; McKemmish, 2001).

The unified model of records management offers a good basis for understanding the interrelationships between businesses, records and archives and sets a framework for standardization, interoperability and co-ordination of records management, not limited by time or space (Hofman, 2004).

3   Research has played a major role in developing industry-accepted standards for electronic document management systems (EDMS), electronic records management systems (ERMS) or electronic record-keeping systems (ERKMS), and electronic information management systems (EIS), for example, in the USA, DOD5015.2-STD at www.dtic.mil/; in the UK, Functional Requirements for Electronic Records Management Systems at www.nationalarchives.gov.uk/recordsmanagement/; in Canada, Request for Proposal: Records, Document, Information Management System: integrated document management system for the government of Canada at www.pwgsc.gc.ca/rdims/ and in Australia, Request for Tenders for VERS Compliant Recordkeeping System Part B: Specification for VERS Compliant Recordkeeping System at http://www.prov.vic.gov.au/vers/compliance/, the European Model Requirements for the Management of Electronic Records at www.cornwell.co.uk/moreq.html and Recommendations for the Effective Management of Government Information on the Internet and Other Electronic Records at http://whitepapers.zdnet.co.uk/0,39025945,60144483p-39000960q,00.htm.

4   Research has had a worldwide impact on establishing international standards for records management. The examples are ISO 15489-1:2001, *Records Management Standard*; ISO 23081:2003, *The Records Management Processes Metadata for Records* (draft); and ISO 14721:2002, *The Open Archival Information System (OAIS) Reference Model*.

5   Research has promoted international guidelines for managing electronic records, e.g. *Guide for Managing Electronic Records from an Archival Perspective* (ICA, 1997) and *Electronic Records: workbook for archivists* (ICA, 2004). The latter draws on professional experience and contributions from international projects in the field of archives and records

management, in particular the work of ISO/TC46/SC11 and the InterPARES project (ICA, 2004).

6 Research has been an integral part of the exchanges of experience and knowledge about records and archives management; it has thus fostered education, training and further research. Research results can be seen at professional conferences, in professional journals and books, and in education and training manuals and programs (An, 2000; Gilliland-Swetland, 2004).

The above analysis indicates the role of research in electronic records management in terms of the development of resources and of contribution to the research process.

Stages of research development and its key features

An analysis of 71 research projects on electronic records awarded by the NHPRC from 1979 to 2002 at http://www.archives.gov/nhprc/projects/electronic-records/projects.html shows that since the first project, dealing with the management of machine-readable records, was awarded in 1979, numbers of research projects in electronic records management have increased, particularly after 1990 (six projects in the 1980s, 39 projects in the 1990s, 24 projects from 2000 to 2003). The first national research on electronic records was carried out in 1991 (Hedstrom, 1991) by the US National Historical Publications and Records Commission (NHPRC). This work was reviewed and revised in 1996 and in 2003 (www.mnhs.org/preserve/records/eragenda.html). Much other research has been done under the guidance of the NHPRC in North America. Its projects include those of Pittsburgh and Indiana Universities, the State Archives of Michigan and the San Diego electronic records project, the University of British Columbia and International Research on Permanent Authentic Records in Electronic Systems (InterPARES).

A study of the subjects of the above projects and of research papers published in professional journals shows the hot topics of research in electronic records management at different periods of time, which reflect the development of research in electronic records management. The development of these research projects falls into three stages according to their research focus.

1 The 1980s: research projects dealt with developing data-processing archives and records management programs for managing machine-readable records in computer-assisted management systems, such as the University of Wisconsin-Madison's project (1980), developing procedures to schedule, accession and retrieve information from machine-readable records of Wisconsin state agencies (www.archives.gov/ nhprc/projects/electronic-records/projects.html.) The research focuses were managing electronic records as electronic data by means of computers.

2 The 1990s: research projects dealt with developing functional requirements for recordkeeping in electronic information systems and in office automation systems (Hedstrom, 1997; Marsden, 1997; Bantin, 1997). The research focuses were managing electronic records as electronic evidence facing the challenges of information technology (State Archives Bureau of China, 1999).

3 The 2000s: research projects concerned the development and promotion of integrated best-practice models, policies, programs, education and training for recordkeeping and archiving in web-based, interactive, dynamic information systems for e-government, e-business and e-commerce (An and Wang, 2004b; Gilliland-Swetland, 2004). There were also projects to develop interoperable recordkeeping metadata standards for complex integrated information systems (Evans, McKemmish and Bhoday, 2004; workshop at www.erpanet.org/, dissemination at www.interpares.org/ip2/ip2_dissemination.cfm?proj=ip2/). The research focuses are managing electronic records as digital information resources and assets with considerations of a variety of contextual factors (including cultural, political, economic, social, technological, legal, religious) at the given time and at the given place (An, 2004a; Wang, 2003).

General directions of the research agenda in electronic records management

The above development of research processes reflects the roles of research in the professional discipline in meeting the challenges of the wired global world. A study of the 71 research projects cited above (www.archives.gov/ nhprc/projects/electronic-records/projects.html), the Electronic Records Agenda Project Final Report published by the NHPRC at www.mnhs.org/ preserve/records/eragenda.html in 2003 and subjects discussed at professional conferences in 2004 (An and Wang, 2004a, 2004b), as well as some of the individual and institutional websites, show some of the changes of the research agenda in electronic records management, and possibly the future direction of research in electronic records management as well. These include the following observations:

1   Types of research have tended to change from the simple to the complex, covering problem-solving, theory-building and test-bed research; descriptive, exploratory, analytical and predictive research; basic and applied research; theoretical and practical research, and so on.
2   The aims of projects have changed from those simply benefiting records and archives management services to those benefiting multiple services to internal and external customers of e-government, e-business, e-commerce, or customers of the digital city and society.

    One of the examples is the International Records Management Trust (IRMT) and the World Bank's collaborative project 'Evidence-based Governance in the Electronic Age' at www.irmt.org/evidence/index.html, which supports governance and service of democracy.

    Another example is the DIRKS manual developed by the National Archives of Australia in co-operation with the State Records Authority of New South Wales. Its 2000 version, *Designing and Implementing Recordkeeping Systems: manual for Commonwealth agencies* (National Archives of Australia, 2000), was primarily aimed at providing practical guidance on managing business information and records for government agency records management project teams and consultants. Its 2001 version, *A Strategic Approach to Managing Business Information* (National Archives of Australia, 2001), provides a flexible methodology that can be applied at different levels depending on the particular needs of an agency. It may be applied to the whole organization or confined to specific recordkeeping systems, business activities or business units, depending on the nature of the particular recordkeeping project. Its 2003 version, *Strategies for Documenting Government Business* (State Records NSW, 2003), is concerned with building more efficient and accountable business practices through the design and encouragement of good recordkeeping.
3   The objectives of research projects have changed not only just for long-term preservation of electronic records, but also for sustainable and

consistent records and information management services throughout the life of a record and throughout the information continuum regime, particularly focused on adding value to business. There has been a change of emphasis from a focus on the medium to the integrated management of electronic records as evidence, information, historical sources, memory, culture, knowledge and information assets; from managing the physical entity to managing its content, context, structure and presentation; from the discrete management of electronic documents or electronic records systems to the integrated management of documents, records, information and knowledge; from managing data to managing the content of web-based resources; and from managing description to managing metadata schemes.

The UK *e-Government Policy Framework for Electronic Records Management* (www.nationalarchives.gov.uk/electronicrecords/pdf/egov_framework.pdf) is a good example of employing electronic records management as a key technology underpinning electronic government, managing electronic records as valuable corporate information resources, encouraging the adoption of cross-government standards for metadata and interoperability to support greater commonality and inter-department working in electronic document and records management, and in the sharing and exchange of electronic records between government systems.

Another example is the ANSI/AIIM/ARMA TR48-2004, *Framework for Integration of Electronic Document Management Systems and Electronic Records Management Systems* (Sprehe, 2004), which allows organizations to cut costs and improve customer service, enabling the vital links between people, processes and projects in a way that empowers organizations to more effectively realize the value in their information assets.

4   Interdisciplinary, multidisciplinary and cross-disciplinary approaches to research form an integral part of any research methodology if stakeholders are to be satisfied with the products of such research. They are no longer discrete approaches to specific problems, but have moved to study the integrated conceptual frameworks dealing with inter-disciplinary, cross-disciplinary and multidisciplinary approaches to broad topics. The Chinese project 'Research in integrated management and services of urban development records, archives and information'

is an example that employs customer-relationships methodology, postmodern archival thinking, the records continuum regime and a total quality management approach to build an integrated framework for the integrated control of services, processes and products of electronic records management services in the urban development field, with the aim of providing client-satisfactory records management, cost-effective and efficient records management processes and good quality of records throughout the lifespan of the records and throughout the lifespan of the built environment itself (An, 2004a, 2004b).

5   There are increasingly needs for pluralism of research methods in professional development. Many modern methods are now used in the development of research.

Taking the Australian Monash University's Clever Metadata Project as an example, methods of conceptual modelling, literary warrant analysis, mapping metadata, meta modelling and empirical instantiation have been used. Conceptual modelling of records in their business and socio-legal context is being undertaken to provide the conceptual framework for the project; analysis of literary warrant is being carried out to discover authoritative sources for the specification of recordkeeping metadata; an iterative process of conceptually mapping the elements of the Recordkeeping Metadata Schema against elements in existing 'best practice' generic sets and elements in recordkeeping-specific metadata sets is being undertaken; modelling of metadata elements is done using two formal modelling techniques: the Resource Description Framework (RDF) and Object Role Modelling (ORM); and empirical instantiation is used by populating metadata elements with examples to highlight inconsistencies or gaps in the metadata syntax and semantic expressions within the set and also to provide guidance to potential implementers on the application of the metadata syntax (www.sims. monash.edu.au/research/rcrg/research/crm/researchmethodology.html).

Another example is the InterPARES project where cross-disciplinary and multimethod approaches have been used, for instance literature analysis, comparative analysis, diplomatic analysis, statistical analysis, survey, field investigation, interview, case study, prototyping and modelling techniques.

6   Groups involved in research have been expanded from records and archives specialists to include new and broader partnerships and

collaborations across disciplines, boundaries and cultures. In McKemmish's (2000, 353) analysis, the experience of a range of research and development projects in the Australian recordkeeping community, such as the Strategic Partnerships with Industry Research and Training (SPIRT) scheme and the Cooperative Research Centres (CRCs) project, she pointed out that the nurturing of collaborative research and development initiatives has been a key strategy of the recordkeeping community in its efforts to develop policies, standards, systems and tools for electronic recordkeeping. Increasingly, this collaborative research is becoming more international and multidisciplinary in nature.

7   Research outcomes have changed from single one-time products to sets of sustainable, coherent and consistent integrated products, adding value to common understandings, information sharing, co-ordination, collaboration and partnerships. These are directed towards the long-term preservation of authentic and reliable electronic records over the entire lifespan of data and information and their effective use by all types of stakeholders and potential clients.

A good example is the UCLA's 'Information Technology and Policy Curricula based upon Electronic Records Management and Preservation Project' at http://polaris.gseis.ucla. edu/swetland/nhprc.pdf, taking a range of stakeholders in aspects of electronic records management and preservation of digital materials into consideration for overall purposes. As Gilliland-Swetland wrote in her NHPRC's proposal (2001), the project concentrated on how undergraduate and graduate education in computer science, information science, information policy, archival science, preservation management, business and law can be used to prepare the next generation of professionals in a variety of fields who will be facing issues associated with electronic records management and information technology implementation in general.

8   The impact of research has broadened from purely local scope to national and international. It has added value to models, programs, technologies, policies and standards, both for specialists and in outside professions. It has spread through questions of communication and education as well as participating in research activities in other fields, to help creators, users, system designers and custodians to build their capacity to manage electronic records and to demonstrate their skills (An, 2003, 70–1).

To equip future records managers with problem-solving abilities for professional success and future leadership in this rapidly changing and volatile environment, research is a key instrument for experimenting, inventing, changing, and improving professional education (Ketelaar, 2000, 322). Integrating research requirements and opportunities at masters and doctoral levels in postgraduate archival education seems a new dimension for building capacity for research. The funding of PhD students seems a global trend to meet the high demand for faculty positions. They are increasingly sought also by industry and the policy development arena for research and development positions (Gilliland-Swetland, 2000, 258, 270).

To expect the unexpected in this networked global society, it is significant to accumulate, share and exchange research experiences in electronic records management across cultures.

Key elements in the success of the InterPARES projects

The above studies mentioned only a few research projects in electronic records management that have made particular contributions to the professional discipline. It is clear that there are some good research projects in electronic records management, but it is not possible, within this chapter, to cover a range of the major projects that highlight aspects of research practice in electronic records management.

The author has therefore concentrated on the InterPARES projects because of their representative range of elements and examples of good practice, being internationally recognized as successful and being transparent in their methodology and the entire research processes. So, what are the key elements in their success, and what can we learn from their experience? A comparison of research components of InterPARES I (findings of the InterPARES project at www.interpares.org/book/index.cfm) and InterPARES II (dissemination at www.interpares.org/ip2/ip2_dissemination.cfm?proj=ip2/) and their relationships indicates that there are five key elements in their success:

1   The aim of the research was to achieve sustainable and consistent development in electronic records management. The projects were closely related to previous and subsequent research and were built on prior work. InterPARES II (2001 to 2006) was based on InterPARES I (1999 to

2001) available at www.slais.ubc.ca/research/current-research/ interpares.htm, and InterPARES I was based on the UBC project (1994 to 1997) available at www.interpares.org/UBCProject/ index.htm. The objectives were clear and relevant. The objectives of InterPARES I and II took forward the management of already existing electronic records to the management of electronic records yet to be created. There was a progression from static databases and document management systems to interactive, dynamic and experimental systems; from a narrow administrative environment to broader artistic, scientific and government environments; and from the processes of records preservation to the processes of creation, presentation and use.

The projects' coverage was inclusive, coherent and rigorous. InterPARES I included requirements for establishing the authenticity of records, appraisal criteria and methods, methods of preservation, a framework for the formulation of strategies, and policies and standards for long-term preservation. InterPARES II dealt with terminology, policy, description and modelling.

2   This research was conducted within a framework of multidisciplinary methodologies. The aim of InterPARES was to develop the theoretical and methodological knowledge essential to the permanent preservation of authentic records generated and/or maintained electronically, and, on the basis of this knowledge, to formulate model policies, strategies and standards capable of ensuring that preservation. Several methods were used, including diplomatic analysis, modelling, surveys, experimental testing, prototyping, and procedural testing. In addition to model policies, strategies and standards, many products resulted from these projects as spin-offs. The methodology consisted of a comparative examination of the relevant literature in the fields of textual criticism and art restoration (www.slais.ubc.ca/research/current-research/interpares.htm).

Four methodological principles were developed by the InterPARES II project (available at www.interpares.org/ip2/ip2_methodological_ principles.cfm). These were interdisciplinarity (with a contribution from several disciplines); transferability (findings can be translated into the language and concepts of each discipline that need to make use of them); openness (InterPARES 2 works as a 'layered knowledge' environment); and multipurpose design (each case study was carried out using

processes of developing research projects and how they can contribute to the international records community. Nothing is known about the relative successes of research projects and the implications of these for future research. This chapter tries to fill in gaps in the literature with a systematic examination of four main issues:

- significant roles and benefits of research in professional development
- stages of development of research processes and their research focuses
- general directions of research in electronic records management
- keys to the success of the internationally known InterPARES projects.

Significant roles and benefits of research in professional development

Research in the field of electronic records management has made significant contributions, bringing six notable benefits to the international records and archives community.

1   Research has provided a variety of methods to increase our knowledge of archival theory and our concepts of records, and broader ways of thinking (but with common understanding) about electronic records as evidence, information and memory. Typical cases are deductive methods in the diplomatic field in the UBC project (Duranti, 1995, 1998; MacNeil, 2000) as a basis for establishing the integrity and authenticity of records, and inductive methods for functional requirements in recordkeeping in the Pittsburgh project for the study of variables in legal, administrative and other organizational operations (Barata, 1997; Bearman, 2003; Duff, 1997, 1998; Cox, 1997, 2000).

2   Research has been used in all stages of the decision-making process to define problems and to identify opportunities, to diagnose causal factors and to clarify alternatives, to evaluate current programs and to forecast future conditions. A variety of management models have been developed for recordkeeping and archiving in a digital context. Two representative management models are the records continuum model at Monash University and the unified model by Hofman, deriving benefit from his partnerships in many international research projects.

The records continuum model provides a concept of service to users throughout the lifetime of records. Its standards-compliant

the methodology and the tools that the dedicated investigating team considered most appropriate for it).

3   In these projects, the researchers had international, interdisciplinary and collaborative customer relationships. The projects were therefore eligible for support from multiple funding and institutional sources.

InterPARES II aimed to develop and articulate the concepts, principles, criteria and methods that can ensure the creation and maintenance of accurate and reliable records and the long-term preservation of authentic records, in the context of artistic, scientific and government activities that are conducted using experiential, interactive and dynamic computer technology.

Scholars in the arts and sciences, archivists, artists, scientists, industry specialists and government representatives from around the world have worked together to meet the challenge presented by the manipu-lability and incompatibility of digital systems, technological obsolescence and media fragility and to guarantee that society's digitally recorded memory will be accessible to future generations. Stakeholders have included individual records creators, organizations, governments, archivists and any other professionals, researchers in all scientific disciplines, the citizenry at large and the information technology sector (www.interpares. org/ip2/ip2_index.cfm).

4   The research results have added maximized value to theory and practice in electronic records management. Some of these are:

- methodology and principles for usable models, programs, technol-ogies, policies, standards, common architectures, interoperability and partnerships in electronic records management
- collaboration with other research projects and standards committees
- contributions to a common core of knowledge for education and training
- better communication between participants, using travel, meetings, discussion and evaluation, websites, conference papers, workshops and publications
- a broader audience and cross-disciplinary readers
- invitations to multidisciplinary and international events
- a prestigious reputation worldwide.

5 The projects were planned with the ideal of integration in mind in relation to the following aspects :

- appreciation of the needs of the different stakeholders involved
- integration between research questions and activities
- consideration of all aspects of project management
- co-ordination between procedures and activities with a time schedule
- co-ordinated teamwork under the project committee, supported by full-time trained researchers
- co-ordination of components of the research with the design of research plans, for example objectives, questions (problems), hypothesis (conceptual framework), methods and methodologies, expected benefits, outcomes and output, findings, dissemination, delivery and publication, the impact of the research, and vocabulary.

Conclusion

This chapter has provided a brief overview of research in electronic records management conducted since 1979. The review has been organized to show the range of considerations that need to be addressed for the future direction of research into electronic records management. Four main issues confronting research projects were considered in turn: significant roles and benefits of research; stages of the research development process and their research focuses; the general direction of the research agenda; and key elements in the success of the InterPARES projects.

As the overview indicates, first, research projects have played important roles in the development of electronic records management and have brought six significant benefits to the international records and archives professional community. It is essential for the continued vitality of professional work that there should be further research projects. Research is a management tool needed for making the right decisions. Records and archives professionals have to work in a competitive environment. A dynamic and changeable digital society is constantly making demands on their competence.

Second, the development of research projects in electronic records management has fallen into three stages. The variation of focus from period to period has depended on the information technology available and the demand for research experienced at the time.

Third, the study indicates that the research agenda for electronic records management requires a methodology integrated with other services. This is the overall direction of all this work. An integrated methodology means collaborative ways of thinking, aimed at guaranteeing the long-term use of reliable, authentic and complete electronic records, and at maximizing the long-term preservation values of the various needs of many disciplines; in providing consistent and sustainable recordkeeping services to meet a variety of users; and in promoting professional commitments and value-added contributions for best practice. Collaborative methodologies focus on positive, rational, interactive, complementary, harmonious and cohesive ways of thinking, rather than passive, irrational, stagnant, incongruous, incompatible or disparate ones. They rely on similarities rather than on difference, on valuing the contribution of different professions and disciplines rather on excluding other potential representatives from a broader society, in government agendas (An 2004b, 129–30): 'Team-work is the great essential of the network society' (Cook, 2001, 278).

Finally, five key elements in the success of the InterPARES projects throw light on the mechanisms of their research practice. Integrated methodologies are important mechanisms in this. Considerations on integration include five components: research purposes, research process and methodology, the research team, research outcomes and research design.

In conclusion, research is a process of enquiry and investigation; it is an endeavour to discover new or collate old facts and reach new conclusions and increase knowledge; it is systematic, critical and methodical. There is an increasing demand for integration methodologies in electronic records management; there are increasing demands for better practice in research projects in electronic records management; and there are increasing demands for education and training in research skills for practitioners, researchers, educators and students. The experience gained from research projects provides directions and best practice about the research that should be incorporated into future projects to improve the quality of the results and to increase their impact on organizations and in the professional community.

References

An, X. (2000) Research in and about Archival Education, *SOA Newsletter*, (UK) **125**, 5-6.

An, X. (2003) Changes and Directions in Archival Research: the influence of Michael Cook's publications in China. In Procter, M. and Williams, C. (eds), *Essays in Honour of Michael Cook*, Liverpool, Liverpool University Centre for Archive Studies (LUCAS), 63-72.

An, X. (2004a) Theoretical Framework for Integrated Management and Services of Urban Development Records, Archives and Information, *Archives Science Bulletin*, **2**, 88-92.

An, X. (2004b) Research in Integrated Management and Services of Urban Development Records, Archives and Information and the Implications. In An, X. and Wang, S. (eds), *Research in Integrated Management and Services for Urban Development Records, Archives and Information*, Beijing, China Architecture and Building Press, 114-30.

An, X. and Wang, S. (2004a) *Research in Integrated Management and Services for Urban Development Records, Archives and Information*, Beijing, China Architecture and Building Press

An, X. and Wang, S. (2004b) The 15th ICA Congress and its Implications, *Archives Science Bulletin*, **6**, 88-90.

Bantin, P. (1997) NHPRC Project at the University of Indiana, *Bulletin of the American Society for Information Science & Technology*, **23** (5), 24.

Barata, K. J. (1997) Functional Requirements for Evidence in Recordkeeping: further developments at the University of Pittsburgh, *Bulletin of the American Society for Information Science & Technology*, **23** (5), 14-17.

Bearman, D. (2003) Can Office Automation Systems Produce Electronic Evidence? In He, J. (ed.), *Proceedings of Office Automation System and Archival Electronic Records Management*, Zhejiang, China, Zhejiang University Publishing House, 9-17.

Cook, M. (2001) The Direction and Role of the Archival Profession, *Proceedings of the First PhD Forum on Archives*, Beijing, China, Publishing House of Renmin University of China, 262-80.

Cox, R. (1997) More than Diplomatic: functional requirements for evidence in recordkeeping, *Records Management Journal*, **7**, (April), 31-57.

Cox, R. (2000) *Managing Records as Evidence and Information*, Westport CT, Quorum Books.

Cox, R. J. and Samuels, H. (1988) The American Archivist's First Responsibility: a research agenda to improve the identification and retention of records of enduring value, *American Archivist*, **51**, 28–42.

Duff, W. (1997) Warrant and the Definition of Electronic Records: questions arising from the Pittsburgh Project, *Archives and Museum Informatics*, **11**, 223–31.

Duff, W. (1998) Harnessing the Power of Warrant, *American Archivist*, **61**, 88–105.

Duranti, L. (1995) Reliability and Authenticity: the concepts and their implications, *Archivaria*, **39**, 5–10.

Duranti, L. (1998) *Diplomatics: new uses for an old science*, Lanham MD and London, SAA, ACA and the Scarecrow Press.

Evans, J., McKemmish, S. and Bhoday, K. (2004) Create Once, Use Many Times: the clever use of recordkeeping metadata for multiple archival purposes, www.wien2004.ica.org/imagesUpload/pres_174_MCKEMMISH_ Z-McK%2001E.pdf [accessed 1 September 2005].

Gilliland-Swetland, A. (2000) Archival Research: a 'new' issue for graduate education, *American Archivist*, **63** (2), 258–70.

Gilliland-Swetland, A. (2001) *Information Technology and Policy Curricula based upon Electronic Records Management and Preservation*, http://polaris.gseis.ucla.edu/swetland/nhprc.pdf [accessed 1 September 2005].

Gilliland-Swetland, A. (2004) *Building the Research Infrastructure in Archival Education*, www.wien2004.ica.org/imagesUpload/pres_388_GILLILAND_ SWETLAND_SAE05.pdf [accessed 1 September 2005].

Hedstrom, M. (1991) Understanding Electronic Incunabula: a framework for research on electronic records, *American Archivist*, **54**, (Summer), 334–54.

Hedstrom, M. (1997) Building Record-Keeping Systems: archivists are not alone on the wild frontier, *Archivaria*, **44**, (Fall), 44–71.

Hedstrom, M. (2004) Why Research is Essential for Teaching and Applications, presentation given at the Asian-Pacific Conference on Archival Education, Beijing, China, 17–19 April 2004, unpublished.

Hofman, H. (2004) A Unified Model for Managing Records, a presentation given at the 15th ICA Congress on 25 August 2004, unpublished.

ICA (1997) *Guide for Managing Electronic Records from an Archival Perspective*, Paris, International Council on Archives.

ICA (2004) *Electronic Records: workbook for archivists*, Paris, International Council on Archives.

Ketelaar, E. (2000) Archivistics Research Saving the Profession, *American Archivist*, **63** (2), 322-52.

MacNeil, H. (2000) *Trusting Records: legal, historical and diplomatic perspectives*, London, Kluwer.

McKemmish, S. (2000) Collaborative Research Models: a review of Australian initiatives, *American Archivist*, **63** (2), 353-67.

McKemmish, S. (2001) Placing Records Continuum Theory and Practice, *Archival Science*, **4**, 333-59.

Marsden, P. (1997) When is the Future? Comparative notes on the electronic record-keeping projects of the University of Pittsburgh and the University of British Columbia, *Archivaria*, **43**, (Spring), 158-73.

National Archives of Australia and the State Records Authority of New South Wales (2000) *Designing and Implementing Recordkeeping Systems: manual for Commonwealth Agencies*, Canberra, National Archives of Australia.

National Archives of Australia (2001) *DIRKS: a strategic approach to managing business information*, Canberra, National Archives of Australia [known as DIRKS Manual], www.naa.gov.au/recordkeeping/dirks/dirksman/dirks.html [accessed 1 September 2005].

Pemberton, J. M. (1992) The Importance of Theory and Research to Records and Information Management, *ARMA Records Management Quarterly*, **26** (2), 46-50.

Sprehe, J. T. (2004) A Framework for EDMS/ERMS Integration, *The Information Management Journal*, **38** (6), 54-62.

State Archives Bureau of China (1999) *Introduction to Electronic Records Management and Archiving of Electronic Records*, Beijing, China Archives Publishing House.

State Records New South Wales (2003) *Strategies for Documenting Government Business: the DIRKS Manual*, Sydney, State Records New South Wales, www.records.nsw.gov.au/publicsector/DIRKS/final/title.htm, and www.naa.gov.au/recordkeeping/dirks/summary.html [accessed 1 September 2005].

Upward, F. (1996) Structuring the Records Continuum Part One: post-custodial principles and properties, *Archives and Manuscripts*, **24** (2), 268-85.

Upward, F. (1997) Structuring the Records Continuum Part Two: structuration theory and recordkeeping, *Archives and Manuscripts*, **25** (1), 10-35.

Upward, F. (2000) Modelling the Continuum as Paradigm Shift in
    Recordkeeping and Archiving Processes, and Beyond: a personal reflection,
    Records Management Journal, **10** (3), 115–39.
Wang, J. (2003) *Managing Essential Information for Organizations in E-age*,
    Beijing, China Archives Publishing House.

Chapter 6

Technologies for preservation

RICHARD J. MARCIANO AND
REAGAN W. MOORE

Introduction

The InterPARES project (www.interpares.org/) has defined some of the essential requirements for a viable preservation environment. The two concepts of authenticity and integrity are used to express the differences between preservation and simple collection building. Authenticity is the assertion that information about the creation of a record can remain associated with the record throughout the preservation life cycle. Integrity is the assertion that a record can continue to be displayed and manipulated in the manner intended by the original creators. Integrity has associated connotations that the bits that represent the record have not been corrupted, that the management of the record can be audited and the custodians identified, and that the archival processes that have been applied to the record can be tracked.

Preservation can be applied to any digital entity, the string of bits that are generated by a computer program. In the diplomatics field, digital entities correspond to records on which actions are based. The records could be files from office products, images, diplomatic communiqués, or more complex products such as e-mail with attachments. Each of these types of digital entities requires a supporting software and hardware infrastructure for its display and manipulation. The supporting infrastructure may be a file system in which the output from a proprietary office product was stored. The challenge that the archivist faces is that the software and hardware environment that is chosen to provide the long-term preservation is rarely the same as the infrastructure used by the original creator of the record. Archival preservation is the process of extracting a record from its creation environment and migrating the record into the preservation environment (Moore, 2004).

The preservation process must contend with inadequacies in current storage technology. The preservation metadata used to describe authenticity and integrity are normally not maintained by storage systems. Thus information about the creator of a record, the institution that sponsored the creation of a record, or a checksum that can be used to validate the integrity of a record are not stored as attributes in the storage repository along with the record. The preservation environment includes not only storage repositories for the records, but also storage repositories for the preservation metadata. The technology that is used to support the preservation environment must link metadata stored in databases with records stored in archival storage systems, and maintain the link through all future upgrades of the software and hardware technology.

A metric for the success of a preservation environment is its ability to manage a set of records independently of the chosen technology. A preservation environment is viable if its digital holdings can be extracted and migrated into a new preservation environment without compromising either the authenticity or integrity of the records. The same capability can actually be incorporated directly within a preservation environment using data grid technology. This is known as infrastructure independence (Moore et al., 2000). Data grids support the migration of digital entities onto new technology through the use of storage and database abstraction layers (Baru et al., 1998; Moore and Baru, 2003). A data grid is able to support a collection of digital entities that is distributed across multiple types of storage systems, with the preservation metadata stored in a variety of types of databases.

We will describe technologies for preservation that are in use today across a wide scale of collection sizes. The preservation technology has been used to support terabyte-sized collections (one terabyte is 1000 gigabytes), and collections with tens of millions of files, as well as collections that have a few hundred files and are a few gigabytes in size. Examples of large collections include the Electronic Access Project (EAP) image collection for the National Archives and Records Administration (NARA) (Moore, JaJa and

Chadduck, 2005) and the National Science Digital Library (NSDL) persistent archive (www.nsdl.org). The NARA collection contains over one terabyte of data. The NSDL persistent archive holds over 25 million files. Both of these projects use data grid technology to manage the digital holdings.

We will also present an example of the migration of the preservation metadata for the EAP collection onto new database technology and the migration of the holdings of an electronic records application into data grid technology. In each case, the metric of success is that after the preservation process, the authenticity and integrity of the original digital holdings can still be verified.

Preservation technology

Let us look at the key concepts behind preservation: authenticity, integrity and infrastructure independence. Each of these concepts imposes constraints on the types of technology that can be used to build a preservation environment. The management of authenticity could be achieved by packaging the preservation metadata directly with a digital record, and storage of the result in an Archival Information Package (AIP) as a file in a storage system. The Open Archival Information System (OAIS) model specifies the contents of an AIP, along with submission information packages for the accession of digital entities and dissemination information packages for the access of digital entities (ISO 14721:2003).

One would hope that an AIP would ensure the link of preservation metadata with the digital record, and thus assure the authenticity of the digital record. In practice, additional preservation metadata is needed that is inextricably decoupled from the AIP. To understand what additional metadata is needed, we need to look at the infrastructure that supported the creation of the original record. The left hand side of Figure 6.1 shows the name spaces that are supported by typical storage systems. These naming conventions provide a way to identify the location where the record was created (typically a network internet protocol address), a way to identify the file (typically a directory path name and a file name), a way to specify some file properties (typically size, creation date, modification date), a way to identify persons who are allowed to access the storage system (typically account IDs), and a way to specify constraints on access to the file (access control lists). These name spaces must be managed along with the records and their authenticity and integrity metadata. An

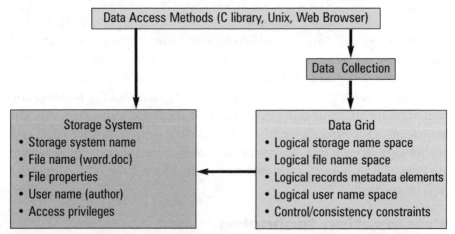

Figure 6.1 Software infrastructure used to support creation of digital
entities, and the mapping to the software infrastructure
needed for a preservation environment

archival information package must be augmented with a supporting
infrastructure that manages all five name spaces to ensure the ability to locate
a file and control the operations performed upon the file.

In practice, one would like the preservation environment to own and
control each of the file naming conventions, such that the naming
conventions would not change when new software and hardware systems
were added to the preservation environment. At supercomputer centres,
which aggressively track technology evolution, hardware and software
systems have a lifetime of about three years after which they are replaced
by new technology. As an example, the archival storage systems used at the
San Diego Supercomputer Center were originally based on the Common
File System technology developed at Los Alamos National Laboratory.
Over a period of 18 years, the archival storage system was replaced by
DataTree software, then UniTree software, then the High Performance
Storage System from IBM, and now a Sam-QFS archive is used that was
developed by Sun. In each case, the change in technology required
specification of a new storage location, a new naming convention for the
files, and a new naming convention for users. A viable preservation
environment would associate standard naming conventions with the digital
holdings that could be maintained and preserved independently of the
naming conventions required by a particular storage repository.

The right hand side of Figure 6.1 lists the logical name spaces that are implemented in data grid technology. For each of the name spaces provided by the original storage repository, a data grid provides an equivalent name space that is now under the control of the preservation environment. This means that the names used to describe files no longer will change when the file is moved onto a new storage system, even a storage repository that is located at a remote site. The distinguished name space used to identify archivists can remain invariant, such that access controls based on archivist names and logical file names still apply as the file is moved to new sites or storage systems. The preservation environment controls the metadata elements that are associated with each file, making it possible to add preservation administrative metadata that are needed by a viable preservation environment.

Let us look at some of the preservation administrative metadata. A good example is the ability to mitigate risk of data loss through replication of digital records. If the copies are kept at a remote location, on different vendor products, and managed by a separate set of administrative procedures, the risks of media failure, systemic vendor product failure, operational error and natural disaster can be minimized. If a third copy is kept in a deep archive, which does not allow access by remote users (typically through the requirement of an explicit staging process for import and export of files), then risk associated with malicious users can also be mitigated. The information about the location of the copies, the validation of the copies through checksum creation, and the status of synchronization of copies can now be stored as metadata that are associated with the logical file name of the original record. The name spaces provided by the data grid ensure that the context used to organize and manage the records in the preservation environment can be kept self-consistent over time. All operations upon the records are carried out on the logical name spaces. The data grid interprets each operation, maps the operation to the actual site at which the record resides, monitors the success of the operations, and updates the associated administrative metadata. The ability to maintain authenticity is built into the data grid as a primary design requirement.

The components of a data grid are shown in Figure 6.2. A key requirement for integrity is to ensure that the standard operations that are performed upon a record are still applicable even when new technology is incorporated into the preservation environment. Data grids accomplish this by separating the operations used to access storage systems or databases from the

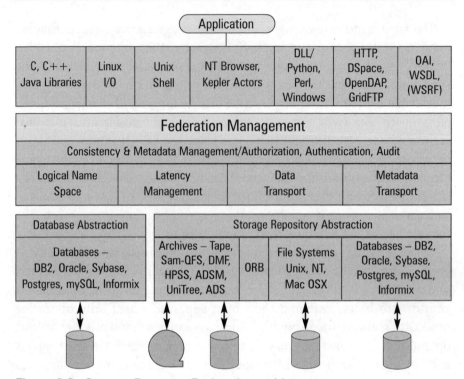

Figure 6.2 Storage Resource Broker data grid components

operations used to present and manipulate records. Standard sets of storage operations are implemented as low-level drivers. This is software that translates from the standard operations to the protocol required by a particular vendor product. The standard operations are based upon those provided by file systems, such as open, close, read, write and so on. The standard operations are augmented by procedures that support access to binary large objects in databases, tables in databases, and objects in object ring buffers (for real-time sensor data manipulation). In addition to a set of standard operations for manipulating files in a storage system, data grids also provide a standard set of operations for manipulating a catalogue stored in a database. The standard database interface includes the ability to import and export XML files, extend a schema with user-defined attributes, support user-defined tables for hierarchical schema, support automated generation of SQL, and support remote application of SQL statements. This makes it possible for the preservation environment to manage the preservation metadata in a wide variety of database technologies.

The separation of the access mechanisms from the management of digital entities in storage repositories makes it possible to port new access mechanisms over time. A standard set of operations that can be performed by an access mechanism is maintained. As new access mechanisms are developed, they are ported onto the standard operations. This means that it is possible to add new technologies such as the DSpace digital library (www.dspace.org) on top of the data management infrastructure provided by the data grid. The preservation environment can add new technology to support more sophisticated access mechanisms without having to modify the technology used to interoperate with storage systems or databases.

The management of integrity requires more than the ability to replicate files to multiple locations. The integrity of the metadata must also be preserved. A simple way to do this is to build upon the concept of federation. A data grid uses a database to manage state information about all of the digital entities that are being preserved. If the contents of the database can be replicated onto a different database product, then the preservation environment can be assured that information such as checksums can be recovered even if one of the metadata catalogues is lost in a natural disaster. A federation of data grids corresponds to the establishment of trust mechanisms on how each of the five name spaces will be shared. The archivist may choose to build three independent data grids, with the first (primary) data grid serving as the master environment. The logical file name space, logical user name space and metadata elements can be cross-registered into the second (secondary) data grid, along with copies of the digital entities. Federation then implies that either data grid could be accessed to discover a preserved record. The federation mechanisms ensure synchronization of the name spaces at periodic intervals under the control of the archivist.

A third data grid could be treated as a deep archive. All interactions with the third data grid would be staged through an archivist-driven procedure. No direct interaction would be permitted between the deep archive and the primary and secondary data grids. The deep archive is in essence a proof that the preservation environment is viable. The only way to populate the deep archive is to extract the entire preservation holdings from their supporting infrastructure, move the holdings to the new site, and then re-implement a new preservation environment that contains only the transmitted holdings. In effect, the preservation holdings will have been extracted from their original preservation environment and migrated onto a new preservation environment. A deep archive that is dynamically created provides the essential proof that a preservation environment is viable (Ludäscher, Marciano and Moore, 2001).

Preservation of authenticity metadata

The process of extracting preservation metadata from its original support environment and migration onto new technology deserves additional consideration. How does one understand the completeness and integrity of preservation metadata associated with electronic records?

The NARA EAP collection presents a rich research opportunity to develop and apply metadata management strategies for heterogeneous collections. Our approach builds on the very impressive work conducted at the Institute for Advanced Computer Studies (UMIACS) at the University of Maryland by Mike Smorul, Joseph JaJa, Fritz McCall and Susan Fitch Brown, in collaboration with Rick Lopez and Bob Chadduck from NARA (Smorul et al., 2003). The UMIACS team conducted a recovery operation on old media and developed a persistent archive demonstration. The additional work described in this paper consisted in relinking all the images to their original archival descriptive context. This work was carried out in collaboration with Mark Conrad at NARA and Mike Smorul at UMIACS.

Between 1997 and 1999, 124,000 records were digitized from a rich cross-section of NARA holdings, including images from 146 record groups and 1056 series.

In spring 2005, the amount of archival materials described in ARC (NARA's current online catalogue) represents roughly 40% of all holdings and is described in the first column of Table 6.1. The EAP NAIL metadata we worked with is described in the second column and illustrates why this collection is indeed such a rich cross-section of existing holdings. Finally, the third column is a reflection of those archival materials that are actually linked to the EAP images (a subset).

Each image may have descriptive metadata at several levels of the descriptive hierarchy (record group/collection, series, file unit, item) and for each level of description different metadata elements may be populated. The research challenge was to relink each image to its corresponding hierarchical descriptive context.

Table 6.1   EAP Image collection – count of descriptive records across the hierarchy

	ARC holdings (as of 11 March 05)	EAP NAIL holdings	Pruned EAP collection
Record group	478	436	146
Collection	788	449	109
Series	12,493	5,386	1,056
File unit	322,532	101,021	2,047
Item	246,985	106,503	73,041
Audiovisual item		5,268	0
Object		23,617	123,361

NAIL metadata

The legacy descriptive metadata we used was based on NARA's Archival Information Locator (NAIL). NAIL metadata was recently replaced by another, closely related standard: Archival Research Catalog (ARC; www.archives.gov/research/arc/). Both NAIL and ARC descriptions are based on NARA's Lifecycle Data Requirements Guide (LCDRG; www.archives.gov/research/arc/lifecycle-data-requirements.doc). LCDRG contains data elements developed for the archival description portion of the records lifecycle, and associates these elements with many different hierarchical levels of archival materials from record groups to items. Archival records are described at the following levels of aggregation:

- record group or collection
- series
- file unit
- item or audiovisual item
- digital object.

Descriptive elements are defined at various levels of this hierarchy. In addition, physical occurrence (PO) and media occurrence (MO) elements can be associated with series, file unit and item or audiovisual item descriptions, in order to further describe the physical and media characteristics of archival holdings. The first four levels roughly correspond to the familiar ISAD(G) international description levels of fonds, series, file and item (ISAD (G), 1999).

LCDRG thus defines a preservation metadata hierarchy. An analysis of the EAP metadata based on the NAIL files identified the presence of multiple variations within the LCDRG metadata hierarchy. This is trivially understandable as objects that are not audiovisual in nature will have no audiovisual metadata.

Each level of the organizational hierarchy has a different set of associated preservation metadata. A collection that is assembled by combining records from multiple record groups, like the EAP collection, will therefore have wide variation in the authenticity information associated with each record. The analysis of the EAP collection was simplified by creating a characterization of the actual metadata hierarchy used across all records, followed by a characterization of the actual metadata present at each level of the hierarchy across all records. The characterizations were a data-driven validation of the preservation metadata, comprising an exhaustive examination of every metadata occurrence.

Given these characterizations, normal database tables were then automatically implemented that could manage the metadata for any of the images. In effect, it was possible to design a single set of database tables that could be used to preserve all of the EAP metadata, while respecting the organizational hierarchy of the original record series from which the images were extracted.

The following steps were taken:

- Flatten the metadata hierarchy (record group or collection, series, file unit, item, audiovisual item, physical occurrence, media occurrence and digital object) and associate the actual hierarchy with each image. This created a list of hierarchies for all objects that could then be analysed.
- Parse the list of metadata hierarchies and generate a pattern (regular expression) that represents all structural metadata organizations present across the entire EAP collection.
- Flatten the metadata hierarchy and associate the presence of each metadata element with the level of the hierarchy and the described image. This created a list of all metadata associated with each level of the hierarchy and of each image.

- Parse the metadata list and create a pattern (regular expression) that represents all metadata that were present within a given level of the hierarchy.

A Perl-based validation 'Regular Expression' tool was developed to create the characterizations of the metadata. All occurrence strings at each level of description of the hierarchy were accumulated. A regular expression that characterizes all instances was then derived.

The resulting regular expressions were used to identify classes of anomalies in the metadata, including artefacts introduced by the archival processes that generated the NAIL files. Examples of classes of anomalies included:

- cases in which a subset of the objects had a unique characterization different from the majority of the objects
- cases in which incorrect metadata tags were present in the NAIL files
- cases with missing metadata or missing objects.

The last case is easy to illustrate, and is a fundamental consistency requirement for any collection. Within the EAP collection, there are:

- 123,602 'Master' TIFF files
- 123,630 'Access' type files
  - 118,120 GIF and 5510 JPEG files
- 123,630 'Thumbnail' GIF thumbnail files.

The number of master TIFF files in the EAP collection is less than the number of JPEG or GIF Access or Thumbnail files. This implies that either 28 master TIFF files are missing, or multiple JPEG, GIF Access and Thumbnail files are associated with a single master TIFF file.

Regular expressions were generated that described the preservation metadata for each level of the organizational hierarchy. The regular expression described whether a metadata item is:

- always present (metadata identifier listed)
- possibly present with zero or one occurrence (metadata identifier followed by a '?')

- possibly present with zero or more occurrences (metadata identifier followed by an '*')
- present with one or more occurrences (metadata identifier followed by a '+').

Example NAIL file

A typical NAIL file (see Figure 6.3) would consist of a variety of linked descriptive records (MTLD refers to the level of description, TI to the title, GRNO to the record group number, NEWTI to a new descriptive section, ENDTI to the end of a descriptive section, NEWSE to the start of a new series, NEWOBJ to the start of an object descriptive section, and ENDOBJ to the end of an object descriptive section). Series-level records are linked to top-level collection or record group records. File unit or item records are

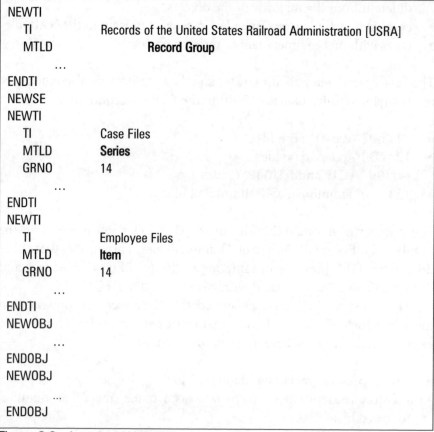

Figure 6.3 A typical NAIL file

linked to series; item records can also be linked to file unit records; and finally object records are linked to item records.

By abstracting the previous sequence as a list of linked descriptive segments, we can summarize it as a hierarchy labelled as: RSIOO (meaning a record group section followed by a series section, followed by an item section and two object sections).

Exhaustively collecting all such observed sequences, leads to a database of linked hierarchical strings. Consider for example the hierarchies:

(1) RSIO
(2) CSIOOIOOOIOOOO
(3) RSFIOIOO

A pattern (regular expression) can be derived, which summarizes all observed sequences:

S(F*(I+O+)* | I+)*)+ (where S=Series, F=File Unit, I=Item, O=Object)

The above regular expression captures all admissible sequences found at the series level.

Once we had characterized the general structure of the hierarchical descriptive metadata, we proceeded to apply the same technique at each level of the hierarchy.

For example, the regular expression that was generated at the record group level (one of the simpler ones) is listed below. Each preservation metadata item is represented by a truncated name. The record group regular expression is given by:

Ti Mtld Grno (Date)? (Tcsd)? (Tcsdq)? (Tced)? (Tcedq)? Tisd (Tisdq)? Tied (Tiedq)? (Fat Fan)* Dcgsd

where the tags in the regular expression have the following meaning:

Ti	=	Title
Mtld	=	Level of Description
Grno	=	Group Number
Date	=	Date Note
Tcsd	=	Coverage Start Date

Tcsdq   =   Coverage Start Date Qualifier
Tced   =   Coverage End Date
Tcedq   =   Coverage End Date Qualifier
Tisd   =   Inclusive Start Date
Tisdq   =   Inclusive Start Date Qualifier
Tied   =   Inclusive End Date
Tiedq   =   Inclusive End Date Qualifier
Fat   =   Finding Aid Type
Fan   =   Finding Aid Note
Dcgsd   =   Data Control Group

Let us now walk through the creation of this regular expression. It was generated by analysing the NAIL metadata records at the record group level of description. Two such NAIL records are illustrated in Figure 6.4.

```
NEWTI
    TI        Records of the Adjutant General's Office, 1780s–1917
    MTLD          Record Group
    GRNO          94
    DATE          Bulk Dates: 1783-1920.
    TISD      1775
    TISDQ     ca.
    TIED      1928
    TIEDQ     ca.
    FAT       Inventory
    FAN       Lucille H. Pendell and Elizabeth Bethel, comps., Preliminary Inventory of
              the Records of the Adjutant General's Office, PI 17 (1949)
    DCGSD         LCS
ENDTI


NEWTI
    TI        National Archives Gift Collection of Materials Relating to Polar Regions
    MTLD          Record Group
    GRNO          401
    TCSD          1750
    TCED          1974
    TISD      1949
    TIED      1976
    DCGSD         LCS
ENDTI
```

Figure 6.4 NAIL metadata records at record group level of description

The derived string patterns are:

Ti Mtld Grno Date Tisd Tisdq Tied Tiedq Fat Fan Dcgsd

and

Ti Mtld Grno Tcsd Tced Tisd Tied Dcgsd

A database of all such record group level NAIL string patterns was built, and the pattern that 'covers' all strings is the resulting regular expression shown earlier.

Several observations are notable:

* We end up with a total of ten regular expressions that provide a 'template' for the entire metadata set: (1) record group, (2) collection, (3) series, (4) file unit, (5) item, (6) audiovisual item, (7) physical occurrence, (8) media occurrence, (9) digital object and (10) the hierarchy itself.
* Single records with isolated errors (appearing nowhere else in the collection) were identified and corrected.

Such regular expressions can be generated for any set of preservation holdings. The appropriate database schema can then be automatically constructed to characterize the hierarchical structure and metadata present at each level of the hierarchy, and the database can then be automatically populated with the preservation metadata. In effect the preservation metadata can be automatically migrated to new technology. This approach also validates the structure of the preservation metadata, analyses the completeness of the metadata, and provides a way to characterize classes of anomalies.

Preservation of electronic records

Given the ability to preserve bits that comprise the digital holdings and the authenticity and integrity metadata, a major challenge still remains in managing the encoding format of the digital entities. Three approaches are currently being researched for how to display and manipulate data:

1   Emulation – the original digital holdings are maintained unchanged.
    The display application is migrated forward in time onto new oper-
    ating systems. This ensures that the digital entities can be presented
    as seen by the creator, but new manipulation technology cannot be
    applied.
2   Transformative migration – the encoding format of the digital holdings
    are migrated to the current encoding standard. This ensures that
    current techniques for viewing and manipulating records can be
    applied. This also helps ensure uniformity of the encoding format
    across the digital holdings. Both the original record and the transformed
    record may be saved.
3   Persistent object – the original digital holdings are maintained un-
    changed. A characterization of the encoding format is created that
    describes the structures, relationships and information content. The
    characterization is migrated over time onto the future syntax for
    describing structure and relationships. A characterization is also made
    of the standard operations that can be supported by the structures
    present in the record. The standard operations are then mapped to the
    capabilities provided by the new display application. This approach
    introduces two levels of indirection between the record and the display
    application; one level of indirection to characterize the encoding
    format, and one level of indirection to characterize the display
    application operations. This makes it possible to change either level
    without affecting the other level. The record may be displayed with the
    restricted set of operations available when the record was created, or
    with the richer set of operations available in the future, provided the
    new operations are mapped to the old structures.

The goals of authenticity and integrity are impacted by the approach
chosen for managing the encoding format of the records. Note that in each
approach, some software component must be migrated forward in time onto
new technology. The emulation approach migrates the display application
to new operating systems. The transformative migration approach migrates
the encoding format of the record to new standards. The persistent object
approach migrates the characterization of the encoding format to new
structure syntax standards. Mechanisms are needed to demonstrate that
the chosen approach does not lose or hide access to the information

content of the record. If a copy of the record is kept in the original format, the archivist has the option to compare results across the multiple approaches at future points in time, and evaluate whether the approach meets authenticity requirements.

The PERM project

The PERM project ('Preserving the Electronic Records stored in an RMA'; www.sdsc.edu/PERM) is an example of the extraction of the structure and information content from a Records Management Application, the characterization of the structure and information content, and the import of the content based upon the characterization into a new Records Management Application. PERM looked at defining a preservation backend for a Records Management Application and demonstrated preservation and interoperability by developing an XML Archiving and Packaging Tool (XAPT).

The PERM project was primarily a collaboration between Caryn Wojcik at the Michigan Department of History, Arts and Libraries and Richard Marciano at the San Diego Supercomputer Center (see project website for a list of all the participants, www.sdsc.edu/PERM/). The State of Michigan had earlier evaluated the capability and viability of using Records Management Applications (RMA) to store, classify and automate the retention of software-dependent electronic records within a centralized repository. While RMAs are capable of retaining and providing access to electronic records, they cannot ensure that the electronic records remain accessible as software becomes obsolete (even if the retention period for the records has not expired yet). In particular, the RMA is not capable of ensuring that they remain accessible as underlying technology changes (word processor formats, image formats, and so on). PERM explored the capability of ensuring that both long-term and permanent electronic records remain accessible.

The project team evaluated the Department of Defense (DoD) Standard 5015.2 for Records Management Applications (version dated June 2002) to develop a standards-based functional map of the features of a RMA that must be retained in the preservation model (http://jitc.fhu.disa.mil/recmgt). This evaluation helped the team isolate the functionality required in the communication between the RMA and the preservation model.

The project team developed 25 functional requirements for a preservation system, and proposed that five functional requirements be added to the

DoD 5015.2-STD to address the preservation of long-term electronic records that are retained in the RMA repository. The functional requirements state that certain attributes of the electronic records should be preserved with the electronic records that are accessioned into the preservation system. Therefore, the project team evaluated the mandatory and optional data elements from the DoD 5015.2-STD to determine if they should be supported by the preservation system. The supported elements were called the 'PERM attributes'. In addition, the functional requirements state that preservation attributes should be created to support administration of the electronic records by the archival repository, and the project team defined what these preservation attributes should be. By doing so, the project team believes that these preservation attributes will be interoperable across various preservation systems.

Finally, through the testing of the PERM functional requirements for preservation, the XAPT prototype demonstrated the migration of RMA records and RMA metadata, and the mapping of vendor-specific RMA metadata into a PERM interoperability metadata schema. This allows for the development of toolkit functionality that operates directly on the vendor-neutral metadata and records. The kinds of transformations the project then demonstrated include: bulk conversion of software-dependent e-mail records into XML, automatic extraction of the original file plan, and standards-based querying of the PERM metadata (using XQuery interfaces).

Summary

Preservation environments are viable if they can control and manage the name spaces needed to describe digital entities. The required name spaces are not only the names of the files representing the digital entities, but also the names of the storage systems, of the archivists who apply preservation processes, of the authenticity and integrity metadata, and of the constraints imposed upon access. Fortunately, data grids provide the ability to separate preservation environments from the choice of software and hardware systems for storing data and metadata. Preservation environments are successful when they can migrate their digital holdings onto entirely new technology while preserving authenticity and integrity.

Acknowledgements

Special thanks to Mark Conrad from NARA and Caryn Wojcik from the Michigan Department of History, Arts and Libraries for reviewing this chapter. This research was supported by the NSF NPACI ACI-9619020 (NARA supplement), the NSF Digital Library Initiative Phase II Interlib project, the NSF NSDL/UCAR Subaward S02-36645, the DOE SciDAC/SDM DE-FC02-01ER25486 and DOE Particle Physics Data Grid, the NSF National Virtual Observatory, the NSF Grid Physics Network, the NHPRC Persistent Archive Testbed (PAT), the NHPRC PERM project, the NHPRC 'Methodologies for Preservation and Access of Software-dependent Electronic Records' project, a.k.a. 'Archivists' Workbench' (where the XAPT prototype was developed) and the NASA Information Power Grid. The views and conclusions contained in this document are those of the authors and should not be interpreted as representing the official policies, either expressed or implied, of the National Science Foundation, the National Archives and Records Administration, or the US government.

References

Archival Research Catalog (ARC), National Archives, www.archives.gov/research_room/arc/ [accessed 1 September 2005].

Baru, C., Moore, R., Rajasekar, A. and Wan, M. (1998) The SDSC Storage Resource Broker. *Proceedings of the 8th Annual IBM Centers for Advanced Studies Conference (CASCON 1998), 30 November to 3 December 1998*, Toronto, Canada.

DoD 5015.2-STD and the list of certified RMAs can be found at http://jitc.fhu.disa.mil/recmgt/UT [accessed 1 September 2005].

DSpace digital repository system, www.dspace.org/ [accessed 1 September 2005].

InterPARES The Long-term Preservation of Authentic Electronic Records: findings of the InterPARES project, www.interpares.org/ip1/ip1_index.cfm [accessed 1 September 2005].

ISAD (G) (1999) General International Standard Archival Description, International Council on Archives (ICA), 2nd edn, adopted by the Committee on Descriptive Standards, Stockholm, Sweden, 19–22 September 1999, Ottawa 2000, www.ica.org/biblio/isad_g_2e.pdf [accessed 1 September 2005].

ISO 14721:2003 *Space Data and Information Transfer Systems – Open Archival Information System – Reference Model*, Geneva, International Organization for Standardization. The OAIS model can also be found on http://ssdoo.gsfc.nasa.gov/nost/isoas/ref_model.html [accessed 1 September 2005].

Lifecycle Data Requirements Guide (LCDRG), National Archives, January 2005, www.archives.gov/research/arc/lifecycle-data-requirements. doc [accessed 1 September 2005].

Ludäscher, B., Marciano, R. and Moore, R. (2001) Preservation of Digital Data with Self-Validating, Self-Instantiating Knowledge-Based Archives, *ACM SIGMOD Record*, **30** (3), 54–63.

Moore, R. (2004) Building Preservation Environments with Data Grid Technology, submitted to *American Archivist*, October.

Moore, R. and Baru, C. (2003) Virtualization Services for Data Grids. In Berman, F., Fox, G..and Hey, A. J. G. (eds), *Grid Computing: making the global infrastructure a reality*, John Wiley & Sons Ltd.

Moore, R., Baru, C., Rajasekar, A., Ludäscher, B., Marciano, R., Wan, M., Schroeder, W. and Gupta, A. (2000) Collection-Based Persistent Digital Archives – Parts 1 & 2, *D-Lib Magazine*, March/April, www.dlib.org/ [accessed 1 September 2005].

Moore, R., JaJa, J. and Chadduck, R. (2005) Mitigating Risk of Data Loss in Preservation Environments, *NASA/IEEE MSST2005, 13th NASA Goddard/22nd IEEE Conference on Mass Storage Systems and Technologies*, April, Monterey, California.

National Science Digital Library (NSDL) www.nsdl.org/ [accessed 1 September 2005].

PERM Project, Preserving the Electronic Records Stored in an RMA, www.sdsc.edu/PERM [accessed 1 September 2005].

Smorul M., JaJa, J., McCall, F., Fitch Brown, S., Moore, R., Marciano, R., Chen, S.-Y., Lopez, R. and Chadduck, R. (2003) Recovery of a Digital Image Collection Through the SDSC/UMD/NARA Prototype Persistent Archive, Technical Report CS-TR-4537, UMIACS-TR-2003-105, www.umiacs.umd.edu/research/adapt/papers/UMIACS-TR-2003-105.pdf [accessed 1 September 2005].

Chapter 7

Legal issues

DAVID O. STEPHENS

Introduction

This chapter is about international laws pertaining to electronic records. Our main focus is to provide a clear picture as to how recordkeeping laws have evolved over time – from the pre-technology era when paper was the sole method of recordkeeping, to the first several decades of computer usage, when paper and electronic records often existed side by side, and finally to the age of the internet and the revolution in e-business, when commercial and other business transactions often occur in a totally paperless environment. Special emphasis will be devoted to the model laws of the United Nations Commission on International Trade Law, as they have been the single most significant factor in the development of international laws connected with electronic records during the past ten years.

Much has been written about the Sarbanes-Oxley Act, which was signed into law in the US in 2002, in the aftermath of such scandals as Enron–Arthur Andersen and WorldCom. This new law imposes rigour and transparency on the management of electronic financial data. Other countries have introduced legislation to address electronic recordkeeping; thus, this chapter aims to take a global perspective concerning some of the key legal issues affecting electronic records and their management.

Let's begin with establishing a basic understanding of the law's interest in organizational recordkeeping. While the law can be bewilderingly complex, it really boils down to a few simple principles. The law's primary interest is that organizations keep and maintain records such that the ends of justice may be served. More specifically, this means that organizations must manage their records in a manner that enables them to demonstrate that:

- the organization is conducting its business with honesty and integrity, and in a manner consistent with the public interest as well as its own
- the organization's records are properly maintained and preserved, in case they may be needed as evidence in government investigations, litigation, audits or other legal proceedings
- the organization is in full compliance with all applicable laws and regulations, in letter, spirit and good faith.

In short, governments everywhere want organizations to manage their records such that they are *complete, true and accurate, accessible, legible, retained as required,* and *fully usable for any and all legal purposes should the need arise.* In practical terms, this means that *any* recordkeeping system, regardless of the particular technology or storage medium employed, should be designed and implemented in a manner such that its operators can demonstrate the integrity of the records if called upon to do so.

Electronic records laws in the pre-internet era

During the first 30 years of computer use, electronic records tended to be used in conjunction with paper records in many recordkeeping environments. Thus, legislative bodies enacted provisions of law that reflected this reality. Let's review some of the most common features of electronic recordkeeping provisions of international laws, most of which were enacted during the pre-internet era of the 1970s through the mid-1990s. While some of these laws have been recently revised or superseded, others remain on the books - with full force and effect - today.

- *Laws pertaining to electronic tax documentation* - Virtually every government throughout the world requires businesses to maintain sufficient documentation to show that all taxes owed have, in fact, been paid. This means that any business records documenting a corporation's tax liability must be properly maintained and fully auditable, regardless of the media on which they have been stored. The tax codes of most countries contain provisions requiring that businesses retain financial and accounting records and other tax documentation for specified periods of time (generally five to ten years), or for as long as they are needed to support tax audits and resolve tax disputes. For example, in the USA, IRS Revenue Procedure 98-25 states that 'all machine-sensible data media used for recording, consolidating, and summarizing accounting transactions and records within a taxpayer's [computer systems] are . . . required to be retained so long as the contents may become material in the administration of any internal revenue law' (US Internal Revenue Service, 1998). Revenue Canada's IC78-10R3 directive contains similar provisions, as does the Australian Tax Office's TR 97/21 directive (Australian Tax Office, 1997; Revenue Canada, 1998).

- *Laws pertaining to record media* – Many countries have enacted laws pertaining to the form or media on which business records may or must be recorded. These laws are relevant in cases where a regulated party wishes to maintain certain records on some non-paper storage media such as microfilm, magnetic or optical media. Usually, these laws do not expressly prohibit the use of these media; rather, they are designed to ensure that, if records are recorded on them, the information will be accessible, legible, accurate and usable for its intended purpose. For example, a now superseded provision of the Danish Bookkeeping Act provides that accounting books and records may be retained on microfilm or digital media; however, these media must be checked for errors and safely kept, while backup copies must be stored separately in a manner that will prevent accidental damage (Danish Bookkeeping Act, 1986).

- *Laws requiring the keeping of 'original' records* – Some countries authorize electronic recordkeeping for certain types of records, but the law contains explicit provisions that the original records must be kept. For example, under the Swiss Code of Obligations, enacted in 1975 and clarified in subsequent regulations, computerized recordkeeping for accounting and tax records is authorized, but the operating accounts and balance sheets must be kept in original paper form (Swiss Code of Obligations, 1975).

- *Authorization for electronic recordkeeping is implied* – The laws of a number of countries contain implied but not specifically expressed authorizations for electronic recordkeeping for certain kinds of records.

Most of these laws apply to accounting and tax records and most indicate that the records may be kept 'in any manner' that will render them fully accessible, accurate and legible. For example, the Audits and Accounts Law of Malaysia makes no specific mention of electronic records *per se*; rather, it states that companies shall cause to be kept such accounting and other records as will 'sufficiently explain the transactions and financial position of the companies . . . and shall cause those records to be kept in such manner as to enable them to be conveniently and properly audited' (Malaysian Audits and Accounts Law, 1996).

- *Requirements to safeguard electronic records against falsification* – The laws of a number of countries contain explicit requirements that companies that wish to create and maintain electronic records must implement measures to prevent such records from being falsified or otherwise tampered with. For example, the Companies Act of South Africa of 1973, as amended up to and through the Revenue Laws Amendment Act 1999, authorizes accounting and tax records to be retained in other than original form, but requires that 'adequate precautions shall be taken against falsification and facilitating its discovery' (South Africa Companies Act, 1973). Similarly, a now superseded provision of the New Zealand Income Tax Act (New Zealand Statues, 1993) provides that where registers, indexes, minute books or books of account are not kept by making entries in a bound book but by other means, adequate precaution must be taken for guarding against falsification and facilitating its discovery. In the discussion that follows, we will see these principles embedded in newer legislation.

- *Requirements that electronic records be printed on request* – The laws of many countries provide that, where electronic recordkeeping is used, the systems must be capable of producing legible paper copies of the records on demand. For example, the Australian Corporations Law of 1989 (revised in 2001) contains provisions authorizing the use of electronic record media in business recordkeeping. However, the information must 'be capable at any time of being reproduced in written form' (Australian Government, 1989).

The modern era: the internet and e-commerce

The World Trade Organization defines e-commerce as the 'production, advertising, sale and distribution of products via telecommunications networks'. In a 1997 policy paper, the European Commission offered an equally broad definition of e-commerce – doing business electronically based on the electronic processing and transmission of data, text, sound and video for many diverse activities, including the electronic trading of goods and services, online delivery of digital content, online sourcing, direct consumer marketing, post-sale services, and other transactions between parties (European Commission, 1997).

But what are the legal implications of doing business in this manner? Many people assume that, in order to be legally acceptable, commercial transactions must be supported by original records and/or authenticated signatures. As we have seen, this assumption is based on the fact that many existing laws were enacted in a pre-technology era, when pen, ink and original paper were the basic 'raw materials' of business recordkeeping as well as the documentation reflecting commercial transactions between buyers and sellers of goods and services. However, in the age of the internet, such 'legacy' recordkeeping practices are no longer sustainable. Thus, new methods of recordkeeping, and the legal basis for them, must be adopted in this new era. The following discussion provides a legal framework for this.

The UN Model Law on Electronic Commerce

In 1996, the United Nations Commission on International Trade Law (UNCITRAL) developed the world's first global legislative model that prescribed legal standards for recordkeeping in 'all-digital' environments. This was the Model Law on Electronic Commerce, and it has revolutionized the laws of electronic recordkeeping throughout the world (UNCITRAL, 1996). This new 'supernational' model legislation was designed for adoption or consideration by the UN's member states worldwide. The basic purpose of the model law is to offer national legislative bodies a set of internationally accepted rules on how existing legal obstacles may be removed, and how a more secure legal environment may be created for conducting business electronically. This model law has been widely adopted, in various forms, by national governments throughout the world, including the US.

With respect to the notions of 'written', 'signed' and 'original' documents, the model law was based on what was termed the 'functional equivalence' approach. This approach is based on an analysis of the purposes and functions of the traditional paper-based requirement, with a view to determining how those purposes or functions can be fulfilled through electronic commerce techniques. For example, among the functions served by a paper document are the following:

- to provide a medium such that a document will remain unaltered over time
- to allow for the reproduction of a document so that each party in a business transaction will hold a copy of the document(s) agreed to
- to allow for the attestation of the integrity of the content of the document by means of a signature
- to provide that a document will be in a form that is acceptable to the courts and other public authorities.

The basic premise of the model law is that electronic records, if managed correctly, can provide the same level of functionality as their paper counterparts. On the other hand, UNCITRAL observes that a digital record, in and of itself, cannot be regarded as an equivalent of a paper document in that it is of a different nature and does not necessarily perform *all* conceivable functions of a paper document. Thus, the model law does not attempt to define a computer-based equivalent to any kind of paper document. Instead, it singles out basic functions of paper-based requirements, with a view to providing criteria that, once they are met by electronic records, enable such records to enjoy the same level of legal recognition as corresponding paper documents performing the same function. The framework of the model law, then, is intended to provide equivalent levels of reliability, traceability and unalterability as would be found in properly managed paper-based systems.

The law applies to any kind of electronic records in the form of 'data messages' used in the context of commercial activities. The term 'data messages' is defined in the law to refer to 'information generated, sent, received, or stored by electronic, optical, or analogous means including, but not limited to, electronic data interchange, electronic mail, telegram, telex or telecopy'. In other words, 'data messages' are, to all intents and purposes, synonymous with the generic term 'electronic records'. The notion of 'data message' as used in the model law is not limited to communication but is also intended to encompass computer-generated records that are used for any business purpose. The aim of the definition of 'data message', UNCITRAL notes, is to encompass all types of messages that are generated, stored or communicated in essentially paperless form. Thus, the notion of 'message' as used in the model law is analogous to that of 'record'. Moreover, the model law includes a broad definition of the term 'commercial activities' – 'matters arising from all relationships of a commercial nature, whether contractual or not'.

For those nations that elect to adopt this model law or some version of it, its provisions will be of especial significance to those engaged in the management of electronic records. The main provisions of this model law that are of direct relevance to the management of electronic records are contained in Chapter II, Application of Legal Requirements to Data Messages, and are summarized as follows:

- *Legal recognition of electronic records* – Chapter II, Article 5, states: 'Information shall not be denied legal effectiveness, validity or enforceability solely on the grounds that it is in the form of a data message.' In 1998, UNCITRAL revised this language to read: 'Information shall not be denied legal effect, validity or enforceability solely on the grounds that it is not contained in the data message purporting to give rise to such legal effect, but is merely referred to in that data message.' Article 9 of the same chapter elucidates this principle further. 'In any legal proceedings, nothing in the application of the rules of evidence shall apply so as to deny the admissibility of a data message in evidence: (a) on the sole grounds that it is a data message, or, (b) if it is the best evidence that a person adducing it could reasonably be expected to obtain, on the grounds that it is not in its original form.' Thus, the model law confers legal status on data messages as business records and further provides for their admissibility as evidence in courts of law, unless there is some reason for not doing so.
- *Legal requirements that information be in writing* – Chapter II, Article 6, provides that 'Where the law requires that information be in writing, that requirement is met by a data message if the information contained therein is accessible so as to be usable for subsequent reference.' This

provision can be construed to provide a general endorsement of new technologies for business recordkeeping, provided that organizations assimilating such technologies adhere to the basic provisions indicated in Article 8, below.

- *Legal requirements for original records* – Chapter II, Article 8, states: 'Where the law requires information to be presented or retained in its original form, that requirement is met by a data message if (a) there exists a reliable assurance as to the integrity of the information from the time when it was first generated in its final form, as a data message or otherwise; and (b) where it is required that information be presented, that information is capable of being displayed to the person to whom it is to be presented.'
- *Criteria for assessing the integrity of electronic records* – Under Chapter II, Article 8, the criteria for assessing the integrity (trustworthiness) of electronic records 'shall be whether the information has remained complete and unaltered, apart the addition of any endorsement and any change which arises in the normal course of communication, storage, and display'. Article 9 elucidates that principle still further: 'In assessing the evidential weight of a data message, regard shall be had to the reliability of the manner in which the data message was generated, stored or communicated, to the reliability of the manner in which the integrity of the information was maintained, to the manner in which its originator was identified, and to any other relevant factor.'
- *Electronic records as a retention medium* – Provisions relating to the retention of electronic records are contained in Article 10 of Chapter II. The important ones are:

(1) Where the law requires that certain documents, records or information be retained, that requirement is met by retaining data messages, provided that the following conditions are satisfied:

(a) the information contained therein is accessible so as to be usable for subsequent reference; and

(b) the data message is retained in the format in which it was generated, transmitted or received, or in a format which can be demonstrated to represent accurately the information generated, sent or received; and

(c) such information, if any, is retained as enables the identification of the origin and destination of a data message and the date and time when it was sent or received.

(2) An obligation to retain documents, records or information in accordance with paragraph (1) does not extend to any information the sole purpose of which is to enable to be sent or received;

(3) A person may satisfy the requirement referred to in paragraph (1) by using the services of any other person, provided that the conditions set forth [in this paragraph] are met.

The UN Model Law on Electronic Signatures

In May 2001, UNCITRAL issued its second major publication concerning electronic recordkeeping – the Model Law on Electronic Signatures (UNCITRAL, 2001). This law provides much more comprehensive guidance for the legislative framework of digital signatures than the brief treatment appearing in the earlier e-commerce law, and is certain to be of equal global significance in the development of international law relative to its subject.

Electronic signatures are defined in the model law to mean 'data in electronic form in, affixed to, or logically associated with, a data message, which may be used to identify the signatory in relation to the data message and indicate the signatory's approval of the information contained in the data message'. To reiterate the need for this legislation, existing country laws impose or imply restrictions on the use of modern means of communication, for example, by prescribing the use of 'written', 'signed' or 'original' documents. In an electronic environment, however, the 'original' of a message is indistinguishable from a copy, bears no handwritten signature, and is not on paper. The potential for fraud is considerable, owing to the ease of intercepting and altering information in electronic form without detection, and the speed of processing multiple transactions. Thus, the objective of this and other digital signature laws and the various technology tools associated with them is to offer the means by which some or all of the functions identified as characteristic of handwritten signatures can be performed in an electronic environment. These functions are:

- to identify a person
- to provide certainty as to the personal involvement of that person in the act of signing
- to associate that person with the content of a document
- an indication of the intent of a person to be legally bound by the content of a signed document
- an indication of a person to attest ownership of or otherwise endorse the authorship of the text and content of a signed document.

Based on these principles, Article 6 of the model law states: 'Where the law requires the signature of a person, that requirement is met in relation to a data message if an electronic signature is used which is as reliable as was appropriate for the purpose for which the data message was generated or communicated.' With respect to the reliability of an electronic signature, the model law enumerates four tests:

1   The signature creation data are, within the context in which they are used, linked to the signatory and to no other person;
2   The signature creation data were, at the time of signing, under the control of the signatory and of no other person;
3   Any alteration to the electronic signature, made after the time of signing, is detectable; and
4   Where a purpose of the legal requirement for a signature is to provide assurance as to the integrity of the information to which it relates, any alteration made to that information after the time of signing is detectable.

UNCITRAL states that the model law is intended to apply where electronic signatures are used in the context of commercial activities. It is not intended to override any existing rule of law for the protection of consumers.

The US E-Sign Law

In June 2000, the US Congress passed, and President Clinton signed, the Electronic Signatures in Global and National Commerce Act – the 'E-sign Act', as it is commonly referred to (US Electronic Signatures in Global and National Commerce Act, 2000). According to many observers, the E-sign Act totally changes the landscape pertaining to the use of electronic information in commercial transactions in the USA. The law does not, however, grant any special status to electronic records *per se*; it merely removes the impediments in existing law to conducting business electronically. In this sense, the law may be characterized as 'media-neutral'. Electronic records will be subject to the same legal scrutiny as physical ones, and the law does not provide any broad authority or mandate for businesses to convert all types of records from paper to electronic format. The law implicitly recognizes that paper records will be used as a medium for business recordkeeping for some time to come. The law provides three key tests for the legal acceptability of electronic records as a retention medium in e-commerce transactions. These are:

- The record must accurately reflect the information contained in the original contract or transaction.
- The record must remain accessible to those entitled by law to access it, for the period required by law.
- The record must be capable of being accurately reproduced, whether by printing or otherwise.

If these criteria are not satisfied, the legal validity of the electronic record may be denied. For records and information specialists, the central issue is whether the organization's e-commerce applications, and the electronic records that comprise them, can be demonstrated to comply with these requirements.

Conclusion: the role of records and information specialists

As is apparent from the foregoing, the central theme of this chapter is the law's requirement that organizations be able to demonstrate that their electronic and other recordkeeping systems are operated with integrity. Records and information specialists have a key role to play in the authenticity and integrity of business records. Indeed, the entire discipline of records management has been characterized as the process of managing the corporate memory in a way that makes trustworthy records readily accessible any time they are required.

The most recent authoritative statements concerning the integrity and authenticity of business records and the role of records and information specialists in supporting it were issued by the International Organization for Standardization, in its international standard for records management – ISO 15489:2001. The ISO standard defines the *integrity* of a record as one that is complete and unaltered. According to the standard, an *authentic* record is one that 'can be proven to be what it purports to be, to have been created or sent by the person purported to have sent it, and to have been created or sent at the time purported'. The record must be genuine and determined to have been managed by specific records custodians through all phases of its life cycle.

To ensure the authenticity of records, the ISO 15489 standard requires that organizations implement and document policies and procedures that are designed to control the creation, receipt, transmission, maintenance and disposition of records. Moreover, the information content of records must be 'protected against unauthorized addition, deletion, alteration, use and concealment'. Moreover, the standard specifies that it is necessary that a record be protected against unauthorized alteration. Records management policies and procedures should specify what additions or annotations may be made to a record after it has been created, under what circumstances additions or annotations may be authorized, and who is authorized to make them. Finally, any authorized annotation, addition or deletion to a record should be explicitly indicated and traceable.

It is the central recommendation of this chapter that records and information specialists work in close concert with lawyers, IT specialists and the business managers having responsibility for recordkeeping systems to achieve these objectives, based on the principles discussed here.

Acknowledgements

The author wishes to extend special thanks to Roderick C. Wallace, CRM, longtime colleague and friend, for contributing to the research for this chapter.

References

Australian Government (1989) *Corporations Act*, Section 288, http://scaleplus.law.gov.au/html/histact/9/4508/top.htm [accessed 1 September 2005].

Australian Tax Office (1997) *Income Tax: record keeping – electronic records*, TR97/21, Canberra, Australia.

Danish Bookkeeping Act (1986) Section 2, Statutory Order No. 60, Chapter 3, Preservation of Accounting Records of Commercial Undertakings, 19 February, Copenhagen, Denmark.

European Commission (1997) *A European Initiative in Electronic Commerce: communication to the European Parliament, the Council, the Economic and Social Committee and the Committee of the Regions*, Chapter 1, The Electronic Commerce Revolution, 15 April. Brussels, Belgium, European Commission, www.cordis.lu/esprit/src/ecomcom.htm [accessed 1 September 2005].

ISO 15489-1:2001, *Information and Documentation – Records Management* – Part 1: General, 1st edn, 15 September, Geneva, Switzerland, International Organization for Standardization, www.iso.ch/iso/en/prods-services/ISOstore/store.html.

Malaysian Audits and Accounts Law (1996) *Companies Act, 1965, Use of Computers and Other Means for Company Records (amended 1996)*, Kuala Lumpur, Malaysia.

New Zealand Statutes (1993) *New Zealand Income Tax Act. Part 10: Administration of companies: company records (articles 189–191)*, Wellington, New Zealand, New Zealand Parliamentary Counsel Office (PCO)/Brookers, 2005, www.legislation.gov.nz [accessed 1 September 2005].

Revenue Canada (1998) *Books and Records Retention/Destruction*, Information Circular No. IC78-10R3, 5 October, Ottawa, Revenue Canada.

Stephens, D. O. (1997) Electronic Recordkeeping Provisions in International Laws, *Records Management Quarterly*, April.

South Africa, Companies Act (1973) *Companies Act No. 61 (sections 85.1, 87.1 and 87.2), Section 105, Register of Members, as amended by the Revenue Laws Amendment Act 1999*, Pretoria, South Africa, www.zadna.org.za/documents/DNA_Articles2.pdf.

Swiss Code of Obligations (1975) *Swiss Civil Code: Book 5: Code of Obligations (Code des obligations). Title 32: Commercial Accounting (De la comptabilité commerciale): Articles 962–3. Amended 19 December*, Geneva, Switzerland: Confoederatio Helvetica (Swiss Federal Authorities), version last amended 3 May 2005, www.admin.ch/ch/f/rs/2/220.fr.pdf [accessed 1 September 2005].

United Nations Commission on International Trade Law (1996) *Model Law on Electronic Commerce with Guide to Enactment*, New York, United Nations Publications, 1999 version with additional article adopted in 1998,

http://www.uncitral.org/uncitral/en/uncitral_texts/electronic_commerce.
    html [accessed 1 September 2005].
United Nations Commission on International Trade Law (2001) *Draft Guide to
    Enactment of the UNCITRAL Model Law on Electronic Signatures*, 17 May,
    New York, United Nations Publications,
    http://www.uncitral.org/uncitral/en/uncitral_texts/electronic_commerce.
    html [accessed 1 September 2005].
US Electronic Signatures in Global and National Commerce Act (2000) Public Law
    106–229, 30 June, www.access.gpo.gov/nara/publaw/106publ.html
    [accessed 1 September 2005].
US Internal Revenue Service (1998) *Revenue Procedure 98-25*, Washington, US
    Department of the Treasury, www.recapinc.com/irs_98-25.htm [accessed
    1 September 2005].

Chapter 8

Ethics and electronic recordmaking[1]

VERNE HARRIS

Introduction: of terms, concepts and plots

When we use (or address) concepts connected to the words 'record' and 'archive' we are, whether we realize it or not, standing above a semantic abyss. Space constraints, and concern for the reader's tolerance, do not allow me to explore this abyss. Suffice it to make a few preliminary observations, as a first movement, on my use of key words. First, my conceptualizations of 'record' and 'archive' are most heavily influenced by the interrogations and uses of the words by Jacques Derrida and Michel Foucault (see, in particular, Foucault, 1992; and Derrida, 1996). So that, for instance, I would happily regard as 'archive' the shared narratives of a collectivity. Second, by 'recordmaking' I understand that huge and messy realm in which what are conventionally called records creators, records managers, archivists, users and so on, negotiate, contest and narrate the meanings and significances of what are called 'records' (see Duff and Harris, 2002, for an extended making of the argument). In this understanding, records are always in the process of being made, they open into (and out of) the future.[2] And by 'politics' I understand an equally huge and messy realm, reaching across orders of the individual and the collective, the personal and the public, in which the dynamics of power and authority engage with issues of principle. In this understanding, the 'political', arguably, coincides with the 'ethical'. In this chapter, for the most part, I have focused my enquiry in terms of narrower categories - on 'records', particularly 'archival records', more particularly 'electronic archival records'; and on the dynamics of power and authority in the public domain, particularly as exercised by structures of the state and of government. The patterns that emerge, I would argue (though space constraints do not allow it), are to be found as well in societal sectors we call 'civil' or 'private'. Clearly, each of these categories also demands semantic sub-enquiry, but to go there would be to risk losing the plot before it's begun (see Harris, 2000, for further exploration of the semantic nuances archived in these words).

A further (de)limitation of my enquiry is constituted by the name 'South Africa'. Rather than attempt to mount my arguments within the impossible reach of the 'in general', I do so out of that geographical space we call 'South Africa'. The analysis perforce embraces the particular, but in drawing conclusions I look always for what we could call the universal. I am not offering a case study; rather, in the specificities of South Africa I look for the play of structural dynamics. The conceptual site for my search is the nexus of recordmaking (specifically electronic recordmaking), archives and the exercise of power. The search reaches from the late apartheid era to the present era of post-apartheid democratization in South Africa. While it unfolds certain significant discontinuities, it also confronts a number of worrying continuities. As Jacques Derrida (2002, 59) has intimated, diagnoses of totalitarian practices can be 'extended to certain current practices of so-called democracies in the age of a certain capitalistico-techno-mediatic hegemony'. The central argument that I mount is that electronic recordmaking – in South Africa, in any country – must always be understood within broader organizational and societal contexts, and that endeavours to promote sound electronic recordmaking are doomed to failure unless they – at least – engage these contexts. I go further, and suggest that these endeavours, ultimately, are political, and that getting the politics right matters more than anything else. What 'getting the politics right' means is, in the end, and in the beginning, a question of ethics.

Historical contexts

We know very little about the apartheid state's deployment of electronic technologies for the purposes of recordmaking. Between 1997 and 1998 the Truth and Reconciliation Commission (TRC) conducted a focused investigation into apartheid-era state recordmaking, with special emphasis on the security establishment. (For a detailed analysis of recordmaking by the apartheid state, see Harris, 2002a.) It revealed only a broad outline of electronic recordmaking, namely, that deployment of electronic technologies became significant in the 1970s, that it gathered momentum in the 1980s driven primarily by the security establishment, and that by the early 1990s in many institutions electronic systems were becoming the primary sites of recordmaking. But three details unearthed by the investigation point to significant underlying dynamics:

- Despite the large-scale destruction exercise mentioned in Harris, 2002a, the TRC team located substantial accumulations of paper-based apartheid-era records. In contrast, the surviving electronic record was sparse. This speaks to two dimensions of electronic recordmaking – the relative ease of erasure and the relative ease of concealment.
- Certain electronic records located by the TRC team were discovered to be unreadable. This speaks to the special challenges posed by the longer term preservation of electronic records.
- While the National Archives (the post-apartheid successor to the State Archives Service) was able to provide the TRC team with a fund of information on apartheid-era recordmaking and opened its doors to a vast collection of paper-based records, it knew very little about electronic recordmaking and had negligible accumulations of archival electronic records.

I want to dwell briefly on this last point. Under apartheid the State Archives Service enjoyed wide-ranging powers over state recordmaking (Harris, 1996). It was also an early user of electronic recordmaking technologies, having introduced automated information retrieval systems in 1974. (For the first two decades these systems were run off STAIRS software.) It would not, then, be unreasonable to anticipate its having secured a handle on state electronic recordmaking by the early 1990s. But for several reasons this was not the case:

- State archivists regarded electronic media as unsuitable for archival preservation – they were acceptable for applications like finding aids (and for bringing efficiencies to process), but not as the bearers of information with archival value. Cut off from international discourse and practice by sanctions, and concentrating expertise in a single division of the organization, the State Archives Service would not accept records for archival preservation in electronic media until 1991.

• In terms of positioning, state archivists under apartheid were subordinate functionaries and bureaucrats within the cultural sector. So that despite their legal powers, they had neither the resources nor the status to challenge powerful agents and agencies. Among the former were IT managers and specialists, who thrived in organizational cultures that privileged 'science', efficiency and technology. Among the latter were those making up the security establishment. Until 1990, both electronic records and the security establishment effectively were placed outside the ambit of the State Archives Service.

The combination of neglect, ignorance, lack of resources, marginalization and deliberate erasure has had dire consequences for South Africa. Two decades of widespread electronic recordmaking by the apartheid state have left almost no residue in archival repositories. And this pattern is replicated outside the state. Researchers intent on engaging our electronic memory resources for the pre-1994 period will find the cupboard almost bare. Extensive databanks documenting natural and human observation, monitoring and surveillance have evaporated. The traces of early word processing, document management and electronic communication systems have gone.

Regime change

If the loss of electronic memory from the 1970s and 1980s has had a severe impact, then a similar loss of memory from the 1990s and 2000s would be disastrous. For the growth in deployment of electronic technologies in the latter period has been exponential. The introduction of PC-based applications in the late 1980s, followed by the internet and integrated office management systems, finally revolutionized recordmaking in offices of the state. While paper and its surrogates will never disappear, today the shape of recordmaking, its heart and its core, are electronic.

While State Archives Service records management archivists did not anticipate this revolution, it was in response to its early rumblings in the late 1980s that they had been pushing for a review of archival policy.[3] That the policy shift on electronic records finally occurred shortly after the state's 1990 unbanning of the ANC and other liberation movements is no accident. The shift was part of a broader process in which the organization's leadership began to acknowledge new realities, accept that fundamental change (whether technological, social or political) was inevitable, and give space to a younger generation of archivists keen to engage international discourses and try fresh approaches to old problems.

The new policy was predicated on a three-pronged strategy (Harris, 2000, 89–91): archival involvement in the design and maintenance of electronic records systems; the earliest possible transfer into archival custody of electronic records with enduring value; and the identification of electronic records that should remain in the custody of creating agencies under the supervision of archival authority. Archival involvement was effected through the building of in-house expertise and the development of appropriate legal instruments. Staff were trained in electronic recordmaking, a dedicated unit within the records management division was established, and when the new National Archives of South Africa Act was passed in 1996 it contained significant and explicit provisions relating to electronic records (Harris, 2000, chapter 10). Soon after the policy shift an agreement was reached with Bureau Nucleus (a substructure of the state central computer service, later named the State Information Technology Agency) whereby the latter would house electronic records transferred into archival custody and provide technical support for their maintenance. By 1994 two electronic records acquisitions had been effected.

In the last ten years the National Archives has focused considerable energy on regulation and standards setting. At the legislative level it has overseen the drafting of provincial archival legislation with provisions for electronic recordmaking, and contributed to the drafting of the Promotion of Access to Information Act (2000) and the Electronic Communications and Transactions Act (2002). In 1999 it published *Guide to the Management of Electronic Records in Governmental Bodies*, which included a standard for electronic records management systems (second edition, 2000, available at www.national.archives.gov.za/rms/gmanerec.pdf). In 2002 it published as a discussion document *Minimum Mandatory Metadata Set*.

The scenario I have just sketched would have sounded like some kind of Eden to those of us who found ourselves in the State Archives Service records management division in the late 1980s. And yet the attributes of Eden end at the list of things that have and are being done. For if we measure the *impact* of these interventions, then we find ourselves in a depressing exercise.[4] Compliance with statutory and other regulatory requirements by state agencies is almost non-existent. National Archives' attempts to educate, monitor and regulate these agencies is reaching only the tip of the iceberg. Its power to approve electronic records systems deployed by the state is almost never exercised. The two electronic records acquisitions mentioned above have not been added to in ten years. (One of the acquisitions, a snapshot of the state-wide personnel administration system PERSAL, has been supplemented by subsequent annual snapshots.) In short, despite the post-apartheid shifts I have outlined, we are looking at a continuing large-scale loss of electronic memory.

Why is this? What has gone wrong? I am naming the need for a diagnosis. But before moving into this space we must pause to examine one further symptom, namely, restriction on public access. South Africa's 1996 Constitution (Section 32) enshrines the right of access to information – uniquely the right applies not only to information held by the state. The Promotion of Access to Information Act (PAIA) was passed in 2000 to give effect to this right, and came into operation in 2001. PAIA has its flaws, but overall it is an excellent piece of freedom of information legislation. The rub lies in its implementation. Because it provides specifically for access to information held in records, it is predicated on sound recordmaking. Agencies with poor records systems, agencies that do not maintain electronic records effectively over time, agencies that do not deploy resources to deal with access requests, such agencies undermine the intent of the law. And both incapacity and a lack of will to implement the law are rampant in South Africa. Another (related) factor is constituted by pervasive cultures of secrecy inherited from the past. Too many information officers reflexively adopt the role of gatekeeper, relying on the prohibitive costs of court action to avoid being held accountable for unreasonable denials of access.

It is difficult to determine trends specifically in the electronic records arena. What is clear is that the systemic barriers outlined above are supplemented by other dynamics: very often requests are dealt with by people who don't even consider what relevant information might be contained in electronic records; older electronic records are often not accessible for technical reasons; and in a country where a relatively small elite has expertise in and access to electronic recordmaking, the medium itself constitutes a significant barrier to access for most people.

A diagnosis

Analysis of the electronic record in post-apartheid South Africa reveals sometimes startling continuities in relation to apartheid-era realities. Electronic memory is still evaporating. While no longer paralysed, the National Archives remains ineffectual. Levels of surveillance by the state remain high. Public access to records is blocked by systemic barriers. The production of public knowledge is skewed by difficulty (sometimes it is an impossibility) in accessing, on the one hand, databanks documenting natural and human observation, monitoring and surveillance, and on the other, evidence of organizational processes. To repeat my questions: Why is this? What has gone wrong?

For some, the answer is a simple one at certain levels of analysis – this is further evidence of the fact that democratization in South Africa has not yet effected fundamental, structural change. I am tempted by this answer, but to stop with it would be to avoid complexity. For the symptoms we discern in South Africa have global dimensions. The disease, if you like, is far bigger than South Africa:

- Despite notable exceptions (national and institutional), and despite continued progress with legislation, standards-setting, software development, and so on, on a global scale the reality is that on the one hand just a sliver of electronic memory is being archived and, on the other, just a sliver of archival memory originates in electronic form (Harris, 2003a).
- Again, despite notable exceptions, national archives around the world remain ineffectual.
- One of the distinctive features of the 21st-century state – and globalization is rapidly creating a universal pattern – is its massive accumulation of information, particularly about its own citizens. It does this both through programmes with a service provision rationale and through the activities of bodies charged with various surveillance mandates. The 'new' information technologies – the pace of their development means that they are always new – provide the state with a capacity for this massive accumulation, which is growing exponentially.
- Although it is not unreasonable to characterize our age as the information age, even as the age of freedom of information, the struggle for public access to information continues around the world. The work of the South African freedom of information non-governmental organizations South

African History Archive (SAHA) and Open Democracy Advice Centre (ODAC) attests to the access challenges facing people even when freedom of information legislation is in place.

So, South Africa is not unique. To return to the terminology of Jacques Derrida, South Africa is part of 'a certain [global] capitalistico-techno-mediatic hegemony'. I will return to this theme in my conclusion.

There *are* South African specificities, and they demand attention. Of course, they are complex enough to require at least an essay-length enquiry. But space is not on my side, so let me offer just an outline of a window into process by focusing on five dimensions informing electronic recordmaking by the state:

- The key auditors of state recordmaking (the National Archives and provincial archives services) are desperately under-resourced. This has to do with questions of status, positioning and strategy (dealt with below), but beneath all of them is the harsh reality that in a country prioritizing redress of past injustice and confronted by challenges like poverty, drought and HIV/AIDS, archival concerns are simply not high on the agenda.

- IT managers and specialists (now often dressed in flashy new names like 'knowledge managers'[5]) remain influential in a country intent on lifting itself into the global mainstream. On the one hand, these players as a rule remain unconcerned about long-term memory, and, on the other, archivists have been singularly unsuccessful in either harnessing or co-opting the leverage that such players enjoy.

- An attribute shared by most national archives enjoying success in meeting the challenges of electronic recordmaking is the degree to which they have been able to imagine and position themselves as more or less autonomous recordmaking auditors. During South Africa's transition to democracy (specifically, during the debates which informed the transformation of South Africa's national archival system), advocates of this approach proved unsuccessful in effecting a meaningful shift.[6] The main obstacle proved to be concern at giving autonomy to institutions still in the early stages of transformation. The result is that – at both national and provincial levels – state archivists remain subordinate functionaries and bureaucrats within the cultural sector.[7]

- South African archivists seeking to address the challenges of electronic recordmaking have too often uncritically adopted strategies that have worked elsewhere. So, for example, they have spent enormous energy in developing standards and regulating the terrain, but have paid little attention either to the political contexts or to the recordmaking cultures they are dealing with.
- South Africa has inherited powerful cultures of secrecy and intolerance for dissent. These cultures flow out of the old apartheid state milieus, the exile experience, and the underground. Moreover, South Africa did not experience a revolution. In transitions from oppressive regimes to democracy, the nature of the transition is critical in determining subsequent access environments. A quick overthrow is the best-case scenario (as happened in East Germany). Protracted negotiated settlements give the oppressive regime time to destroy records and provide the space for more or less secret deals, which stimulate sensitivity to later disclosures,[8] which in turn stimulate concern about the 'danger' of giving state archives their heads.

Conclusion: understanding power

Conventional wisdom suggests that the loss of electronic memory has to do – at its profoundest levels of causality – with the absence of appropriate recordmaking cultures. To use the terminology of Terry Cook (1994), 'paper minds' addressing 'electronic records' is a recipe for disaster. Now, I don't wish to dismiss this analysis out of hand. There is an element of truth in it, and it would be foolish to underestimate the importance of changing 'paper minds'. But I wish to conclude by suggesting an even profounder level of causality. And to do so I must return to the concept archived in the term 'archive'.

It is relatively easy (and therefore frequently done) to make the argument that the very structure of archiving, that the process that is recordmaking, both invites politics in and generates a politics of its own wherever 'archive' happens. Ultimately, there is no understanding of the archive without understanding of politics. But let me briefly go a step further by arguing that politics is archival, that the archive is the very possibility of politics (Harris, 2003b). Let me acknowledge at once that this is not an original argument. Without drawing the conclusions that I do, many archivists have moved into this space, even implied the argument, by pointing out the strong correlation between oppression and thorough recordmaking. To quote Chris Hurley (2001, 1), for example: 'Historically, tyrants have more regard for good recordkeeping than democrats. Totalitarians are notoriously good recordkeepers.' In my reading of archival literature, however, only Terry Cook – in scattered references throughout his more recent work – has suggested that politics is best understood in archival terms. It is no accident that a feature of Cook's work is its openness to discourses outside the narrowly 'archival', in particular to the epistemological moves of the so-called postmodernists.[9] It is from the latter, in particular Jacques Derrida and Michel Foucault, that I derive the argument.

Scholars and commentators from many disciplines and many countries, working with a range of theoretical and epistemological frameworks, have unfolded how the exercise of political power hinges on control of information. My own favourite is Noam Chomsky, whose searing critiques of democracy, in the USA especially, demonstrate how elites depend on sophisticated information systems, media control, surveillance, privileged research and development, dense documentation of process, censorship, propaganda, and so on, to maintain their positions (see, for instance, Mitchell and Schoeffel, 2002). But it is Derrida and Foucault who reach most deeply in exposing the logic, even the law, underlying these phenomena. In the words of Derrida (1996, 4): 'there is no political power without control of the archive, if not of memory.' And Foucault (1992, 129), coming from a different direction but nailing the same law: 'The archive is first the law of what can be said. . . .' And *when* it can be said, *how* and *by whom*. Both of them insist on the archive as a construction, one that issues from and expresses relations of power. Listen to Derrida (Derrida and Stiegler, 2002, 3) elaborating this insistence in relation to media apparatuses:

> Who today would think his time and who, above all, would speak about it . . . without first paying some attention to a public space and therefore to a political present which is constantly transformed, in its structure and its content, by the teletechnology of what is so confusedly called information or communication?

The confusion in this naming of 'information' and 'communication' stems from an underestimation - sometimes an ignoring - of what Derrida (Derrida and Stiegler, 2002, 3) calls 'fictional fashioning': 'No matter how singular, irreducible, stubborn, distressing or tragic the "reality" to which it refers, "actuality" comes to us by way of a fictional fashioning.'

'Information' is always fashioned, always constructed. Derrida clears away the confusion by deploying the term – the concept – 'archive'. In its Derridean deployment, 'the archive' is the law determining meanings and significances; the law, if you like, determining contexts. Here, beneath the surface whirl and clatter of information, is where the instruments of power are forged. Instruments that in their most fundamental of operations create and destroy, promote and discourage, co-opt and discredit, *contexts*. Archivists have conceptualized what they do around their special expertise in context. But it is the *archon*, the one who exercises political power, who is the purveyor of context and who is the archetypal archivist.

I submit that the elites that oversee Derrida's 'capitalistico-techno-mediatic hegemony' – and this could easily be true of all elites – are primarily interested in recordmaking as an instrument in the exercise of power. Concern for good records systems has to do with immediate functional imperatives. Concern for long-term memory and all the concepts, values and processes associated with it – history, heritage, archives, legacy, freedom of information, and so on – does not stretch far beyond the imperative to control contexts. Elites are never interested in what actually happened – it is too complex, messy and potentially explosive – or in creating space for people to contest the past – that leads to dominant metanarratives being challenged. They are interested in shaping the past and containing contestation. We saw this play out in almost exemplary fashion during the build-up to the war on Iraq (2002–3).

This analysis invites archivists to contemplate certain uncomfortable conclusions:

- The most powerful imperative to ensure good recordmaking is constituted by the desire to exercise control. (As I have already pointed out, it is no accident that oppressors are the best recordmakers.) So that recordmakers who extol the value of recordmaking to good governance, to accountability, transparency and so on, are probably undermining rather than promoting their cause.
- It is common cause that long-term memory in paper-based records is still better and more comprehensive than that in electronic records. But it would be a mistake to assume that this has to do primarily with the

relative absence of archival cultures in the electronic domain. A more obvious explanation is that archival cultures are weak across the board, and that the nature of electronic media simply makes it more difficult for archivists to rescue an enduring record.

- Changing 'paper minds' is but the first step in what has to be a long and comprehensive agenda for struggle. Ultimately our struggle is a political one. Polities that care about good governance, that care about justice, also care about history, heritage, archives and so on. Get the policies, standards, techniques and so on right, but ignore the politics, and we are wasting our time. Get the politics right, and all the other elements will want to fall into place.

For archivists and others who care about electronic memory it is time – and it has always been time – to wise up. Good recordmaking seems to thrive in what we could call extreme environments – oppressive environments, on the one hand, and environments shaped by the call of justice on the other. Unless we understand the political dimensions and conceptualize our struggle as a struggle for justice, we condemn ourselves to rearranging deckchairs on a sinking Titanic. Listen to Peggy Kamuf (Derrida, 2002, 21) reading Derrida reading the work of literary theorists: in her reading:

> [Derrida] ties this work to its political responsibilities in the world it is attempting to think, a world whose horizon can only be justice. I would even say that the notion of *oeuvre* being elaborated here must be understood as this work of making connections to a world that *could* still be more just, that is thereby being urged or called to more justice, more justice for all, for all the living and the dead, past and still to come. To put it still more boldly or baldly: the work of the *oeuvre* is justice and resistance to injustice.

Increasingly, in the last decade, Derrida engaged the question of 'archive', and this engagement invites a direct transposition from Kamuf's reading – for Derrida (Harris, 2002b), the work of the archive is justice and resistance to injustice. And to transpose one more time – the work of recordmaking is justice and resistance to injustice. *The* issue in electronic recordmaking is ethics.

References

Cook, T. (1994) Electronic Records, Paper Minds: the revolution in information management and archives in the post-custodial and post-modernist era, *Archives and Manuscripts*, **22**, 2.

Derrida, J. (1996) *Archive Fever: a Freudian impression*, Chicago IL, University of Chicago Press.

Derrida, J. (2002) *Without Alibi*, Stanford CA, Stanford University Press.

Derrida, J. and Stiegler, B. (2002) *Echographies of Television*, Cambridge, Polity Press.

Duff, W. and Harris, V. (2002) Stories and Names: archival description as narrating records and constructing meanings, *Archival Science*, **2**, 3-4.

Foucault, M. (1992) *The Archaeology of Knowledge and the Discourse on Language*, New York, Pantheon.

Harris, V. (1996) Redefining Archives in South Africa: public archives and society in transition, 1990-1996, *Archivaria*, **42**.

Harris, V. (2000) *Exploring Archives: an introduction to archival ideas and practice in South Africa*, 2nd edn, Pretoria, National Archives.

Harris, V. (2002a) The Archival Sliver: power, memory and archives in South Africa, *Archival Science*, **2**, 1-2

Harris, V. (2002b) A Shaft of Darkness: Derrida in the archive. In Hamilton, C. et al. (eds), *Refiguring the Archive*, Cape Town, David Philip.

Harris, V. (2003a) The Challenges of Preserving Electronic Memory Over Time. Delivered at a conference on 'Challenges and Best Practices in Electronic Records Management', convened by Long Sight, Sandton, July 2003.

Harris, V. (2003b) The Archive is Politics: truths, powers, records and contestation in South Africa, keynote address at the conference 'Political Pressure and the Archival Record', University of Liverpool, Liverpool, July 2003, unpublished.

Harris, V. (2003c) After the Hefer Circus, *Natal Witness*, (29 December).

Hurley, C. (2001) The Evolving Role of Government Archives in Democratic Societies, paper presented at the Association of Canadian Archivists' annual conference, Winnipeg, June 2001, unpublished.

Mitchell, P. and Schoeffel, J. (eds) (2002) *Understanding Power: the indispensable Chomsky*, New York, New Press.

Footnotes

1   This chapter was prepared initially as a paper (with the title 'The Record, the Archive and Electronic Technologies in South Africa') for presentation at the annual Society for the History of Technology conference in Amsterdam, October 2004. It has benefited from comments on early drafts by Brad Abbott and Heiko Roehl, and from decisive interventions by the editors of this volume. Nevertheless, I take full responsibility for the 'final' text.

2   It was Jacques Derrida (1996, 68) who coined the phrase 'the archive opens out of the future'.

3   I was an archivist in the State Archives Service's records management division from 1988 to 1994.

4   This conclusion was drawn by Louisa Venter (Assistant Director: Electronic Records Management Programme, National Archives) during discussions at the conference 'Expectations and Realities in Managing Electronic Records', Johannesburg, June 2004. She confirmed it in written responses to me later in June 2004.

5   In my view organizations can manage information, records, people, business processes and so on. They cannot manage knowledge. What is called knowledge management is simply the co-ordinated management of resources and processes.

6   I document this in Harris, 1996. The Truth and Reconciliation Commission also recommended a fundamental repositioning of the National Archives. However, its recommendation lost its force through contradictory elaboration – at one and the same time it advocated independent agency status (the ideal) and positioning within either the office of the president or that of the deputy president.

7   In 2001 the National Archives of South Africa Act was amended by the Cultural Laws Amendment Act. One of the changes tied the National Archives more tightly into the state bureaucracy.

8   In 2003 the proceedings of the Hefer Commission provided a fascinating window into how this sensitivity is playing out in South Africa (Harris, 2003c).

9   The terms 'postmodernism' and 'postmodernist' require problematization – a task beyond the scope of this paper. Suffice it to say that both terms are used commonly to categorize the work of both Derrida and Foucault. In my view neither of them can be described meaningfully as 'postmodernist'.

Chapter 9

Competencies – the asset that counts most: on developing human talents as a prerequisite for successful EDRM changes

THIJS LAEVEN

Introduction

Thinking about training, education, staffing or competencies in an electronic document and records management (EDRM) context has one advantage: there are no standard requirements available on this specific item. Model Requirements for the Management of Electronic Records (MoReq) does not mention terms like education, staff, professionalism, competencies or qualification. There are no relevant statements about the issue in the DoD 5015.2 standard. In fact only the ISO 15489 standard and the ERPANET toolset say something in general terms on training.[1] Is this really an advantage? Or is it a tacit assumption that moving organizations towards these standards can be safely laid in the hands of competent professionals?

Deliberate actions in the domain of human resource management (HRM) are required to develop further the competencies of records management staff who are responsible for implementing organizational change in the context of installing an EDRM system. Change management demands change managers and likewise transforming traditional recordkeeping towards EDRM demands transforming records managers. How should these transformations be managed?

This chapter sketches out a way of dealing with human resource development (HRD) in an EDRM context. Taking my activities as a consultant in EDRM implementation projects as a starting point, I will share some points of knowledge and instruments that I have acquired and tested in my work. I will give a personal view of lessons learned, based on experience and reflection.[2]

HRD matters should not be situated at the end of the bid-and-buy cycle of an EDRM system – which is too often the case. The supplier of course offers some kind of training to support the effective use of the new system. At its best such skills training has very restricted operational objectives ('how to . . .'). It mostly lacks variety in pedagogic formats (it is unidirectional, teacher driven) and pays little attention to differences in learning styles and to the transfer of learning into practice. Training should not be at the bottom of the list.

Instead, learning would be better at the very heart of the innovation itself. In fact innovation means change, changing equates to learning, and learning is the core of HRD. I will consider here the process of innovation in record keeping – for example, the implementation of an EDRM system – as an excellent chance for continuous professional development (CPD) of all those who are involved.

After introducing CPD, I will summarize approaches to change management and then associate it with learning organizations and competency management. Finally, I will structure learning activities in a learning cycle to underline the continuum of learning and developing.

Continuous professional development

First let me explain what CPD means in my view. It is the common responsibility of employers and employees to create and exploit learning opportunities within the working environment with a view to staff career mobility and the dynamics of knowledge sharing.

I will illustrate this with reference to three career steps.

1   The 'junior professional' (in whatever discipline, let us say records management) is the person who is entering her or his first job with a diploma stating a basic or entry level vocational qualification. It is the qualified 'new' professional who must become established by having a programme to settle into the job. This working and learning programme is supervised by a more experienced colleague, separate from ordinary management.

2   The 'midpoint professional' is the qualified employee who works independently to perform the required results and who is fully responsible for the quality of her or his work, according to standards that the organization or peer professionals consider to be average. To achieve this objective a working and learning programme is agreed between the employee and her or his manager as part of a (corporate) professionalization scheme.

3   The 'senior professional' is the highly qualified employee whose performance is considered to be at the top in the field. This person can be a generalist who covers a wide range of activities and responsibilities, or a specialist whose judgement and expertise are recognized to be relevant within and outside the immediate working environment. The senior professional participates actively in professional programmes, most likely as a coach or supervisor.

Figure 9.1 summarizes these job career stages and continuous learning activities. The career path is presented as a straight line in only three steps, which is often not the case. A career has its own pattern and pace, depending on the professional's competencies and ambitions on the one hand and on the organization's needs and possibilities on the other.

Different job profiles reflect these career stages. As far as EDRM is concerned, the path is reflected in typical products and activities. These may include, for example, making inventories of working processes and linking them to folder structure (junior professional), making and revising manuals and job aids (midpoint professional) and policy and strategy making (senior professional).

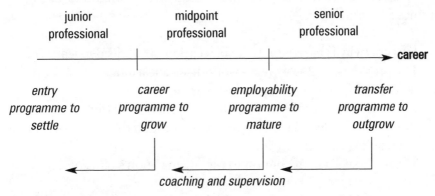

Figure 9.1 Job career stages and continuous learning activities

CPD is just one aspect of human resource management. All HRM activities are intended to achieve a match between the organization's objectives and the individual's ambitions. As far as knowledge-intensive organizations are concerned, they generally try to apply methods of organizational learning. This means fitting learning into working – or the other way around – in order to increase knowledge production and circulation, hence to enlarge competitiveness. Corporate learning is a continuous process as part of the organization's knowledge management. CPD is an investment in human capital, the most valuable asset available. The return on investment is in the quality of the working and learning output. So the visible effect of learning must be a change in professional behaviour. For the individual member of staff, investment is repaid with satisfaction, recognition and employability.

As CPD is the joint responsibility of workers and employers, when it wants to create a lifelong learning environment, the organization offers jobs that challenge employees to apply their skills and to discover opportunities to learn. This creates a culture that allows people not simply to do their jobs but – within given limits – to take risks, to make mistakes. The organization facilitates workers in discovering skills or knowledge gaps and in filling the gaps. For workers, this means that they are conscious of what they do and do not know. They must have a learning competency for themselves and towards colleagues. Knowledge is not a private possession, but it is something to share with colleagues, which is a matter of attitude rather than skill. Learning activities can be formal and informal, depending on whether or not they are planned and structured. They can take place off the job and on the job.

The most important characteristics of the learning continuum are, in my opinion:

- Every activity is based upon the perception of the need to learn (plan).
- The programme closely links working and learning.
- It allows different learning styles (learn).
- Learning makes professional behaviour change (perform).
- Everyone involved in the activity must reflect on the objectives and on the results (reflect).
- They all make a contribution to the organization's objectives.

Models of change management

The models of which I am aware have in common that transformations are based on a solid vision and a widespread sense of urgency. They are well communicated, and learning activities are set up to empower people. Empowerment gives competencies a chance. Continuous education becomes a crucial factor in the success of changes. Continuous education is not merely a matter of publishing one catalogue a year of available training in the market, it is a state of mind and an aspect of the culture in a learning organization.

I will use John P. Kotter's (2002) model to demonstrate that it gives excellent learning opportunities for CPD, taking the changes associated with EDRM as an example. My role as an external consultant involves monitoring the learning process for the change-leading team as a whole and for individual participants. What are their objectives? How do they reflect on the process and the outcome?

In Kotter's view a transformation must be triggered by a widely felt sense of urgency. I like the example of the national defence minister who cannot give an account to parliament of a peace keeping mission, owing at first glance to failing records management. This crisis was a serious threat to the minister's political life. It was an opportunity to increase awareness of risks throughout the organization. The lesson we learned was that methods for physical document management were no longer sufficient to deal with electronic documents and records. It made short work of the idea that recordkeeping is some kind of paper-handling business hidden at the end of working processes, instead of recognizing the strategic value of professional recordkeeping in the digital era. In this case recordkeeping staff proved not to have sufficient qualifications and influence with recordkeeping staff to implement an EDRM strategy.

In Kotter's views the next step is to make a team 'the leading coalition', which is based on personal prestige, network, influence, information, authority, skills and leadership. They are the pioneers who first and foremost trust one another and feel very concerned and very motivated. They can have powerful communication with other people. For the members, teamwork is a matter of action learning. Although the work is done collectively, learning efforts and effects will vary. In the EDRM example, one of the highest ranking executives, as well as advisors, records managers, 'ordinary' workers and end-users, work together.

The next activity is to develop a daring and challenging vision and a strategy for how to reach the future. This is a creative process where several scenarios are proposed and rejected. The vision must be presented in short, appealing images or texts that generate ideas, plans and emotions. The way to create understanding and to give rise to emotions (anger, anxiety, trust, rejection . . .) is part of a communication strategy. In the EDRM project campaigns were created that included videos, meetings, workshops, interviews, seminars, gadgets and pop-ups – all intended to present the message. The force is in the conciseness, the repetition, the reciprocal nature of the message, and in the example of influential people.

As far as the transformation itself is concerned – the strategy leading to the realization of the vision – Kotter would say that empowerment is at the very heart of the change process. It generates support and is the basis for short- and long-term success. It guarantees a continuity of change that anchors innovations in the organization. These are further steps in his model. In the case of the EDRM project this included developing a CPD programme.

How to manage learning within an organization?

At whatever career stage or transformation stage, learning within a changing organization means learning by qualified adult people that must result in behaviour and outputs that fit with the organization's (future) objectives.

Learning is a process of giving meaning to phenomena that occur in your environment. Learning is building a new mental representation of knowledge by associating new information with existing knowledge. Meaningful learning occurs when individuals are engaged in social activities like working. Daily work gives rise to authentic problems. Solving problems rearranges knowledge and produces new understandings. Although this is a mental process, the results will become visible in a new approach to similar or different problems, now and in the future, in other words in new professional behaviour. Different learning styles may lead by different routes to similar solutions.

When unknown problems present themselves, for example, when a new vision demands new recordkeeping techniques, the gap between existing knowledge and skills and required new understanding and behaviour may be too great, or the existing knowledge and routines are an obstacle to gaining new ones. In such circumstances day-to-day on-the-job learning can be insufficient and learning intervention must be 'heavier'; for instance off-the-job training that is designed to fill the gap. Think of traditional recordkeeping personnel who are used to reacting to requests from end-users who come to hand over their documents for filing, or to ask for filed documents to be found. A more proactive behaviour is required. The information needs of the end-user become the priority, and the recordkeeper makes a user profile in interaction with the user. One might imagine a series of steps that gradually lead this person to develop the required attitude and skills. The process might pass through a workshop on tools and techniques, then a safe simulation context where the interaction is with colleagues or a trainer, and finally a more challenging interaction with 'real' users.

Managing the learning process means creating opportunities that challenge employees to bridge the gap between existing knowledge and required new understanding and behaviour. This demands insight into the employee's competencies.

Competency management

Competency management (CM) can be defined as *the measures to ensure that the right competencies are in place at the right moment in the right place.* Of course one can enlarge this definition and replace 'the right place' by 'the right people in the right positions' – which makes clear that CM is one aspect of HRM. The same holds good for determining the moment at which people should hold specific positions, which is a matter of recruitment, staffing, career planning and CPD. This is to say that learning and development must be a planned activity; do not wait until the transformation has taken place before starting a programme. A transformation will certainly fail if development is not a synchronic activity: it is a *conditio sine qua non.*

What remains in completing the definition of CM is a question of the right 'competencies'. In my view, a competency is a combination of knowledge, understanding, skill and attitude that makes a worker's performance visible as successful professional behaviour. A competency may be task-independent or job-related. The question of which competencies are to be considered the right ones is somewhat more complicated.

Figure 9.2 gives an overview of competency development activities. First of all they are embedded in the organization's strategy and structure, which can be stable or under change. The core element is what I call the competency catalogue. This is a survey of the competencies as defined by the organization's objectives. It will contain general – corporate – competencies as well as specific – job-dependent – ones. Both types will be worked out in behavioural indicators. These are overt signs in an employee's behaviour that she or he is learning the required competency.

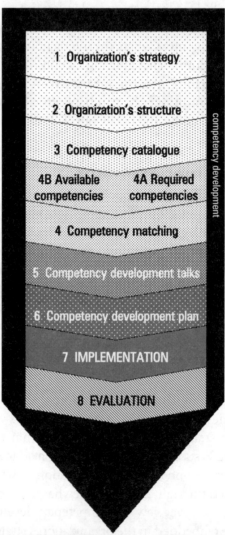

Figure 9.2 Competency development: an overview
© Innogration Management Consultants, Harderwijk, the Netherlands, 2005

Example 9.1 is a part of the job profile for an EDRM advisor in a state ministry. Example 9.2 shows some details of a general competency (part A) and of a job-dependent competency (part B). In many organizations a catalogue of general competencies will be available. As far as the EDRM-specific ones in the Netherlands are concerned an interactive website is available where job-specific competency profiles can be generated.[3]

Example 9.1   Job profile of an EDRM advisor (condensed version)

Position:
Shared Services Facility Management SSF.

Orientation:
SSF customers, at the level of line and project organizations and RM management.

Results:
Advice and instrumentation regarding EDRM at tactical level. Translating EDRM developments into opportunities for directorates and departments. Participation in EDRM consultation at tactical level.

Principal tasks:
A. Develop EDRM expertise and transfer it to RM staff.
B. Contribute EDRM expertise to interdisciplinary working groups and ICT or RM projects.
C. Embed EDRM in primary processes and integrate EDRM in information management.
D. Develop, apply, monitor quality management for EDRM.

Products:
Work instructions, guidelines, job aids, on-the-job training, coaching and counselling of RM managers and staff, brochures, helpdesk and back office, evaluation of and advice on RM applications and tools, implementation programmes, presentations, participation in working groups.

Continued on next page

Example 9.1 *Continued*

Basic competencies:
- problem solving capacity
- interpersonal behaviour
- influencing behaviour
- network power [see Example 9.2A for details]
- organization sensitivity.

Job-related competency [see Example 9.2B for details]:
- thorough knowledge and understanding
- analytic and synthetic skills
- tool development and implementation skills, all regarding EDRM-related ICT, business administration, recordkeeping and archiving, and legal aspects.

Example 9.2 Competency profile of an EDRM advisor (condensed version)

A. Basic competencies (example)

Name	Description	Indicators
network power	develop, maintain, use relationships with a view to obtaining information, support and/or co-operation	• seek and maintain contacts with people in the organization who might be relevant for your own tasks and information supply (also informally) • raise interest of (influential) people for support and collaboration regarding your own
tasks,		propositions and suggestions (also informally) • organize and use (temporary) connections and engagements to reach your own targets and objectives (forge coalitions and alliances)

Continued on next page

Example 9.2   *Continued*

Name	Description	Indicators
		• seek and maintain contacts with your fellow professionals inside and outside the organization who are relevant for your own tasks, growth, development • conduct yourself at ease in existing, new or unknown social and professional environments • bear in mind that networks exist thanks to the principle of rendering services and getting favours in return and behave likewise with respect of ethic and social norms and codes • be aware that networks require maintenance, even when the urgency of co-operation or support has declined • activate or reactivate networks at the right moment

B. Job-related competencies
- thorough knowledge and understanding
- analytic and synthetic skills
- tool development and implementation skills, all regarding EDRM related ICT, business administration, recordkeeping and archiving, and legal aspects.

Examples:

EDRM-related ICT

• ICT systems as usual within state government and ministry • information analysis and data modelling for complex administration systems	*job-specific subjects*: • management of documents, data and databases

Continued on next page

EDRM-related ICT *Continued*

• functional requirements for recordkeeping systems especially digitized	• formats and media for storage conversion, migration and substitution strategies • RM applications and standards • ingestion and capture of documents and (technical) metadata • infrastructure, web technology and data communication • information retrieval and security

Business administration

• mission, tasks, responsibility and processes of state government and ministry • interrelations between primary and supportive systems and processes • co-operation intra and inter-governmentally and (inter)nationally • information and knowledge management and systems • domain and institutional context of the ministry	*job specific subjects*: • system analysis • context analysis • analysis, (re)design, evaluation of processes and procedures • workflow management • knowledge management and technology

EDRM-related recordkeeping and archiving

• sustainability • quality management • management of context and metadata • business process and transaction-oriented recordkeeping and appraisal	*job specific subjects*: • version and platform management • standards like MoD, ISO, MoReq • query languages and technology

Continued on next page

EDRM-related recordkeeping and archiving *Continued*	
	• access, appraisal, recordness, capture, ingest, disposal
	• integrity and authenticity

EDRM-related legal aspects	
• national and specific law and by-law	*job specific subjects*:
• norms and literary warrant	• risk analysis and risk management
• enforcement	• public governance
	• privacy and copyright protection

With these tools it is possible to make job and competency profiles specifically for EDRM jobs. The great advantage of such specific profiles is that employees and managers share a common language to discuss the competencies as these manifest or do not yet manifest themselves through the workers' behaviour.

If these profiles are future oriented they give an image of the required competencies at the end of the ongoing transformation process. They can easily be used to make a comparison between required and available competencies so that discrepancies can be discovered. This can be done in self-assessment, but also as a peer assessment, as a chief–subordinate assessment or any other 360-degree assessment. That is what is called competency matching in Figure 9.2 (page 136). It is not like a test or an exam, which works with objective criteria. The result is a judgement based on intersubjective observations and agreed on by the employee and his or her chief.

The results are input for competency development talks between a manager and her or his subordinates. They can be part of a career or CPD programme and will eventually produce a development programme, for either individual or group. The remainder of Figure 9.2 is about the execution and the evaluation of this programme.

Figure 9.3 (overleaf) shows another possible use of the competencies catalogue. It can serve as a competency-driven personnel planner, which supports the selection of workers who will be (or will not be) placed in future positions. This is an extremely delicate process, even more sensitive than the simple matching procedure. When selection is at stake the development and use of the instruments requires a clear protocol that describes the

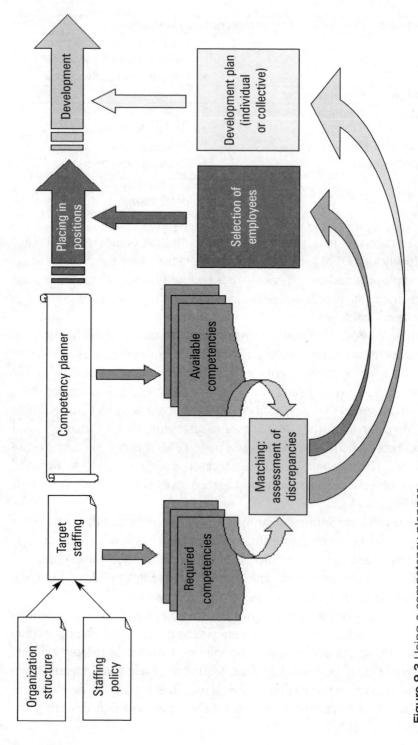

Figure 9.3 Using a competency planner

© Innogration Management Consultants, Harderwijk, the Netherlands, 2005

onditions, the process and the possible outcomes. Such a protocol can best be made by close contact with the people concerned in their roles of employers and employees. The same holds good when making a competency catalogue and matching tools. Even when they are not used as a selection tool, people who work with them for the first time are somewhat apprehensive. This is not really surprising as assessment is implied, which is always a delicate matter. For that reason it is essential to be meticulous, even more so because it is not a matter of passing a multiple choice test for measuring knowledge. The behavioural indicators must be as precise as possible, focused specifically on the people and the organization.

Learning cycle for continuous development

In monitoring learning activities during EDRM implementation processes, the cycle in Figure 9.4 can be of some help to individual recordkeeping staff to organize their professional development. The (self) assessment on competencies and the discrepancies it uncovers is the starting point.

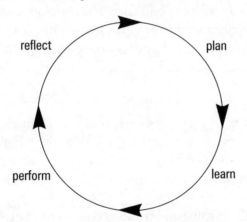

Figure 9.4 The continuum of competency-driven learning (with thanks to W. Edwards Deming)

Plan

This is the analysis phase and the phase of preparing the learning activities. It means looking forward to the changes to be achieved. This is done by making learning objectives concrete and explicit and generating a kind of checklist such as:

- How do I plan to do the learning? (in affordable steps)
- What concrete activities will I be undertaking?
- What results do I want to reach?
- What performance indicators are relevant to acquire which competencies?
- Does my manager (mentor, coach or supervisor) agree with my plan?

One can refer to this checklist during the following steps and write down immediately one's observations and experiences. It serves as a personal logbook, to avoid forgetting crucial information.

The EDRM example above mentioned an off-the-job workshop on tools and techniques, followed by a safe simulation context where the interaction is with colleagues or a trainer or selected users and finally 'real life' interaction with ordinary end-users. For example, this process can be divided into three steps. In the first step a workshop helps to train participants in discussion techniques for the purpose of making a user profile in an interactive way with the end-user. The simulation in the laboratory setting needs preparation: for example, a separate room with video and computer facilities and a schedule of people present (recordkeeper, client, trainer) and an instruction on how to generate and give feedback.

Learn

At this stage the learning activities are executed as planned. In the example this might be the workshop on techniques. When developing or acquiring such activities, the following questions can help to maximize their short- and long-term effect. They also apply to e-learning.[4] Does the activity:

- refer to realistic learning and working contexts and problems (in terms of tasks, roles, responsibilities)?
- make the audience responsible for their own development activities?
- make the organization responsible for creating a suitable learning environment?
- help to achieve behavioural change?
- support self-regulated learning and reflection?
- contribute to developing the organization's learning culture and the individual's learning behaviour?

And how does it achieve these objectives? These questions help to monitor the activities on an individual level (employee and manager) and on a collective level (the organization concerned and the trainers' organization, be it internal or external).

Perform

This stage is a crucial one as the transfer from learning to working must be made here. The success relies heavily on the preceding steps. The behavioural change that was the starting point of the learning activities must be effective here. Performance improvement must become visible and permanent as a sign of a competency that has developed in the required direction. It is at this stage that the return on learning investment must become assessable.

The boundary between 'Learn' and 'Perform' is vague in a learning organization. Crossing boundaries will be gradual, depending on whether the focus is on change and improvement or on production and performance.

Reflect

The reflection phase is often neglected. When performance is achieved, things are thought to be OK. But reflection on learning activities and output gives valuable feedback on the objectives and on the process that has led to reaching them. In the cycle, this phase precedes 'planning'. But in fact the reflection might best be prepared during the planning phase. This is the purpose of the checklist, to which one can refer as a logbook during the following steps. This is the evaluation phase. One must give honest answers to questions like:

- How do the learning activities contribute to my objectives?
- Which activities did so and which did not?
- Why did they?
- What was my own part in the activities and what did other people do?

The more precise the answers are on the subject's experiences, feelings, thoughts and on those of other people involved, the more valuable they are. A logbook like this also helps to prepare evaluation or career discussions. One could also try to obtain feedback from others.

Conclusion

Empowerment of EDRM staff should also include effective policy-making and networking within their organizations. Staff must be capable of taking responsibility for the strategic dimension of the information management of their organizations. In general the situation is that EDRM staff have no access to the CEO level, they have no budgets, they have no influence. They may be happy when a new Document Management System (DMS) or Records Management System (RMS) can be purchased (perhaps even with their involvement in the definition, tendering and acquisition process). But they may then remain silent for the following years, instead of creating awareness of the potential contribution of the data they manage to the knowledge management, the asset management and the risk management of their organizations. (E)DRM must not be situated at the end of the lifecycle of documents, but at the very heart of it. That means gaining and developing other qualifications and attitudes for EDRM staff. They must not merely focus on storage, but be actively involved with the business processes, from the very beginning.

In this contribution I have claimed that organizations that are on the move to meet current EDRM standards can only have competent recordkeeping staff if these professionals play an active role in the development of their required knowledge, understanding, skills and attitudes. They should participate in a continuous learning programme that leads them from the expected competencies to showing new professional behaviour. Critical reflection on (future) tasks and competencies is a prerequisite for finding and exploiting learning opportunities.

This key point can be suitably highlighted 'in conclusion' by citing two crucial studies: 'Human Resources: the critical element', a chapter in Kurtz (2004); and 'Humans – the Ultimate Tool for Preserving Digital Information' by Simon Tanner (2004) of King's College London.

Acknowledgements

I wish to thank Hans Scheurkogel from the Netherlands Archiefschool (Institute for Archival Research and Education) in Amsterdam, president of the ICA section on education and training. He has given feedback on an earlier version of this chapter.

References

Kotter, J. P. (1996) *Leading Change*, Boston MA, Harvard Business School Press.

Kotter, J. P. (2002) *The Heart of Change: real-life stories of how people change their organizations*, Boston MA, Harvard Business School Press.

Kurtz, M. J. (2004) *Managing Archival and Manuscript Repositories*, Archival Fundamentals Series II, Chicago IL, Society of American Archivists, (especially chapter 8).

Tanner, S. (2004) Humans – the Ultimate Tool for Preserving Digital Information, paper given at ERPANET seminar *Business Models related to Digital Preservation*, Amsterdam, Netherlands, 20–22 September, www.erpanet.org/events/2004/amsterdam [accessed 1 September 2005].

Footnotes

1   ISO 15489-1:2001, Part 1, General, section 11, and in some more detail in 15489-2:2001, Part 2, Guidelines, section 6. It is said that an organization must have an 'ongoing programme of records training' addressing all those who create or capture records. ERPANET (www.erpanet.org) has been publishing a series of guidance tools over the last two years. They are all intended to support professionals in implementing new strategies for EDRM. The most recent one is concerned with 'ingest' of digital objects into digital repositories. The tool contains a 'people' chapter. It stresses that 'when building a delicate system, people can cause both success and failure' and it is underlined that 'in a field with such a rapid development cycle, training should not be neglected'. The other tools also pay attention to 'people' or 'roles and responsibilities' in a similar way (refer to www.erpanet.org/ for full details).

2   I have not given an exhaustive list of my sources of inspiration. Many of them are in Dutch. I wish to acknowledge scholars, colleagues and all the record managers and archivists I have had the chance to work with. I will mention the *Handboek Effectief Opleiden*, Reed-Elsevier, the Hague, from 1994, and many of its authors on all aspects of organizational learning. They depart from ideas of renowned specialists like Chris Argyris and Peter M. Senge. I like to reach back to sources like Michel de Montaigne (16th century, France). John Dewe (19th and 20th century, USA) and Philip Kohnstamm (20th century, Holland) for their very inspiring lessons on how individuals learn and develop. I refer to Mathieu Weggemans for his writings and lectures on knowledge management, and to Robert J. Simons

and Joseph Kessels for their ideas on curriculum development and competency management. I wish to mention colleagues and researchers of university schools of archives and records management, especially those of the *Archiefschool* in Amsterdam, and active professionals in this domain, for sharing views and knowledge with me.

3   North-American and Australian standards were of great help in developing the website.

4   Electronic learning environments can be of great help in developing, distributing and to using time- and place-independent educational tools for initial or continuous professional development of records management staff, or for end-user oriented support. But the traditional rule for all kinds of education does not cease to apply in the digital age: the organization must have a learning and training vision and strategy that support the achievement of its goals and targets. [*Education, Training and Operation – from the Traditional Archivist to the Information Manager*, AIIM and DLM White Paper, Hamburg, 2002].

Chapter 10

Records management: two case studies from the French private sector

PIERRE FUZEAU

Introduction

The two case studies chosen deal with the implementation of records management systems in private sector organizations between 2001 and 2004. This is a long-enough period to allow us to draw lessons from the implementation phases and to analyse the results obtained once the systems were fully working. One case concerns a financial institution with over 2500 employees (in the banking sector) and the other a service company with under 50 employees. In the first case records management is applied in the context of optimizing work flows and business processes. In the second case records management is used in close association with a knowledge management approach. Analysis of both cases shows user satisfaction, risk reduction and cost reduction emerging as positive outcomes.

Case study 1: records management and electronic archiving
The context

As in other European countries where national regulations have evolved in line with European directives, the French Civil Code has incorporated a new definition of the written word. Article 1316 of the Civil Code now reads: 'Literal proof, or proof through the written word, results from a series of letters, characters, figures or any other signs or symbols that carry intelligible meaning, irrespective of the medium on which they are carried or their mode of transmission.' Similarly, new definitions of the formats in which evidence can appear are to be found in Article 1316-1 of the Civil Code: 'The written word in electronic form is accepted as proof in the same way as the written word in paper form, on condition that its author can be duly identified and that it has been created and kept in conditions that guarantee its integrity' and in Article 1316-3 of the Civil Code: 'The written word in electronic form enjoys the same force of proof as the written word in paper form.'

The law's technical equivalent had also to be produced to make the law applicable in practice. Thus, the French national standard NF Z 42-013 on 'recommendations for the design and operation of computer systems with a view to ensuring the preservation and integrity of documents held in such systems' appeared in its first version in 1999 and in its second version in 2001. It covers time and date stamping, digitization processes, handling of different media and registering of data, security, operating procedures, audit and outsourcing. It is worth pointing out in this regard that the ISO Standard 15489 on records management (ISO 15489:2001), which appeared in French in 2002, adds matching organizational elements to the technical standard cited above.

In the context of these regulations and standards, the financial organization under consideration saw an opportunity to modernize its system of managing records.

The company employs 2500 staff and has 200 branches, 1.2 million customers, and 2 million accounts. The case was made more complex since four different regional banks, each having different practices and forms, had merged to create this institution. Finally, the establishment was in the process of migrating to a new computing platform. All the factors that bring complexity were present in this records management project.

An analysis of the initial situation showed that the existing records storage premises were full to overflowing and the need to build an additional facility was high on the agenda. On the basis of an annual increase of 10,000 storage boxes – one linear kilometre – with a conservation period of ten years the facility would need to cover an extra 2000 square metres. Very high financial costs were involved in processing archived files (a team of seven staff to register and check agreements) and in desktop publishing (production of print-outs), an increase of 50% over three years. Furthermore, existing problems needed to be addressed: lost agreements (customers had taken a copy of an agreement home to have it signed by a relative and the contract had never been returned, and the organization had failed to request its return) and incomplete or improperly completed agreements (unsigned agreements, for example). Finally, long search and retrieval times no longer satisfied the needs of either counter staff or customers. Waiting times of two to three weeks had been estimated.

Results of the investigations

Six geographically distributed storage sites existed, which was proving very expensive, and volume growth meant that extra space was needed in the short and medium term. If no changes were made, over 50 linear kilometres of additional storage space would be needed. With fairly small changes in organization and the introduction of new technology, studies showed that a stable level of 16 linear kilometres of storage capacity would suffice. This highly impressive result was made possible thanks particularly to the introduction of a business classification scheme and a complete life-cycle table, making it possible to identify every category of document and closely analyse the risks in case of loss.

The business classification scheme showed that 90% of total records fell into only six types of file: securities, loans, agreements, counter documents, cheques and insurance. By examining each of the six collections of documents, the organization's 'vital' activities were linked to files and then to records that were vital to the ongoing existence of the company. These vital records were identified and assessed. For each collection, the potential damage in case of loss was then measured on a case-by-case basis, from both the financial and the legal points of view. Detailed working meetings were held with the disputes, litigation, accountancy and legal departments.

The decision was taken by the directorate immediately to set in motion a project in two distinct parts:

- on the one hand, a shift to electronic processing and storage of cheques, which was outsourced; the existing stored items have a lifecycle of ten years and the stock will therefore be reduced to zero by 2010
- on the other hand, priority was given to moving to a totally electronic environment for signed paper agreements with a view to reducing the high number of mis-matches, saving over 10 linear kilometres of shelving – 1000 square metres of surface area, of redeploying handling staff (from seven down to two), producing very high quality of service to users and customers (in speed of access, accuracy, comprehensiveness of coverage and increased confidence in the system) and, finally,

obtaining a significant financial saving. This move to an all-electronic environment, in view of its higher critical nature, was not outsourced.

Agreements come in every day from each of the bank's 200 branches. The quality and comprehensiveness of the coverage were not guaranteed during this stage. It was after this first stage that the control process applied.

The 10,000 agreements per day each take the form of a number of hand-signed pages. One of the particularities that caused technical difficulties was that each page of the agreement contains one or more subsidiary agreements. A customer may subscribe to three financial products for example and sign a single page on which these three products figure; supporting documents of all kinds may be interleafed between agreements, such as the customer's national identity card and so on. In this way there is no guarantee of the order in which the supporting documents and the agreements appear. These are some of the constraints to be taken into account in the processing of the record throughout its lifecycle.

The implementation of a records management approach

The records management process implemented in this organization within the framework of ISO 15489:2001 and the French standard NF Z 42-013 now authorizes the destruction of agreements in paper form. The complete process of document handling throughout its lifecycle is a records management process. See Figure 10.1.

As soon as the form has been drawn up in the branch, the agreement is registered in the central database as an event. Once the contract is duly signed and approved by the customer, the paper form is filed in a folder, which is then transferred by specialist carrier to the records processing centre.

Once the batches coming from the branches have been checked in by the handling staff in the records management centre, the agreements and supporting documentation are checked (unstapled, unfolded and so on) and immediately digitized on two scanners either of which, for security purposes, can be used as a back-up should the other one fail. The images thus obtained are stored in protected temporary space. The automatic document recognition systems (identification of the agreement number by page and of the category/ies of each agreement) and automatic character recognition systems (reading of account numbers, account names, date, amount, and so on) take over and upload the metadata they have collected into the temporary storage.

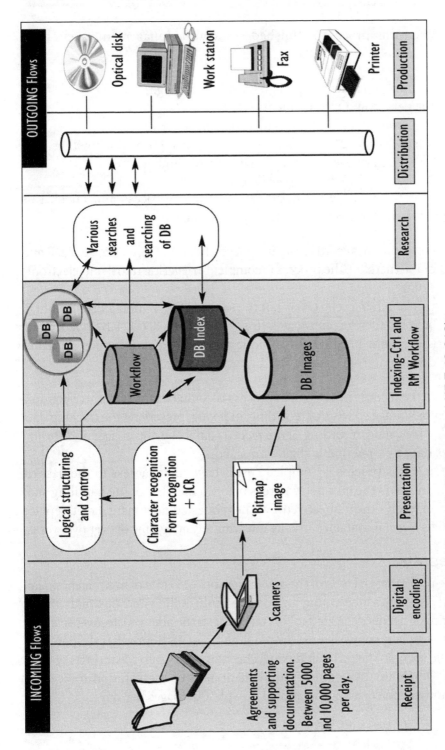

Figure 10.1 EDM Solution – Workflow+RM (standard NF Z 42-013)

When this process is finished, a records management programme processes the following data:

- the images (note: several agreements per image) (IM)
- the data from the agreements (DC)
- the 'event' data from the central database (DE)
- the data on the location of the paper agreements, which will be kept for six months for security reasons (box number) (DB).

The records management software will then process and check this information and produce the following results:

- entry into the records system is successful: DC=DE, existence of DB and of IM, therefore the process is complete, triggering transfer to electronic storage
- mis-match in cycle: DC is not the same as DE, or non-existence of DB or of IM, therefore mis-match (triggering a manual check by videocoding (document imaging) or a request for information or for a further document from the relevant branch).

When the records management process is complete, transfer into electronic records storage consists of recording, indexing, preserving the tracking data in log files, daily recording of the records database, the images and the log files onto non-rewritable digital optical disk.

Once this process is complete, users have direct access to the desired document via the intranet, whereas before a member of the handling staff had to receive the request, retrieve the requested document, fax it, replace it in its original container, usually involving a waiting time of over two weeks.

Results

The performance levels of the system rely on a 1% rate of mis-matches dealt with through videocoding and on the multiskilling and flexibility of the handling agents dedicated to this task and on the ability to access the image of the agreement with a maximum time lag of 48 hours after despatching (time spent in digitizing, indexing, checking, entry into the records system, and 'burning' disk copies). Implementation of the solution took eight months for a start-up operational rate of 5000 pages per day.

The return on investment for a project with a budget of €400,000 (about £275,000) came after two years, taking into account savings in personnel (€150,000 per year) and in space (€200,000 per year in the long term).

Security has been improved threefold thanks to saving and storing on three media instead of a single medium as in the initial configuration.

Paper versions can be destroyed because of the quality and completeness of coverage of the electronic records system achieved by the organizational and technological systems of electronic document management, records management and electronic data storage.

Satisfaction levels among direct users and customer end-users are high because of the reduced transmission delays for document requests and because of reproduction quality.

Case study 2: records management and knowledge management
The context

This case study involves a management consultancy and training company with fewer than 50 staff. Within its own information system the company has embedded knowledge exploitation and knowledge sharing tools. Knowledge flows depend essentially on a groupware solution and are accessible by blocks. This 95% electronic solution is rendered highly secure through its records management processes.

For a consultancy and training company knowledge management is an integral part of business strategy. For its consultancy and training contracts its consultants and trainers need to be constantly aware of the evolving business context since they are coming up against new concepts, new technologies and new regulations (such as recently introduced standards).

In the case under consideration the company's move to new offices in 2001 provided the opportunity for a management decision, after a series of consultations with employees, to implement a real knowledge management system based on records management processes. It re-established its information system from scratch, integrated Lotus Notes, renewed its computer hardware and its networking, integrated high-speed internet access, an intranet and an extranet, all this being specifically designed with the aim of providing company staff with a maximum amount of information and knowledge with the highest level of security.

Objectives

The objectives set for the new information system were of two kinds. The first objective was to make savings in time and personal efficiency, since the year 2000 was when French employment law reduced the statutory working week to 35 hours. In a service company a reduction in the working week can result in a direct loss of turnover, since what is being sold is consultancy days. The group project working inside the company on the 35-hour agreement and the way it was to be applied came to the firm conclusion that information needed to be shared throughout the company more dynamically. The second objective was then, naturally, the exploitation of knowledge. Knowledge is an integral part of all experience amassed on the ground during work on different outside contracts: ratios, feedback, knowledge of client's business, comparative performance of different market systems, test results, and so on.

The intranet platform

Each member of staff is networked, through Lotus Notes, and has access to the whole information system, with a few exceptions, such as accounts and personnel files. The information system as a whole consists of several databases organized in blocks. Some are enriched by interpersonal exchanges between teams and activities by e-mail and electronic discussion groups. Their function is to collect raw information, coming from mailing lists or discussion lists, or picked up in professional exhibitions or conferences, and transmitted internally within the company for qualifying comment. Other blocks , dedicated to the company's own areas of expertise, are broken down into collaborative working spaces (shared diaries and knowledge bases), fed by data and documents drawn up in the context of projects led by different teams and which are limited by access rights: writing and editing rights are limited to the project team; sharing as read-only is for other staff collaborating within the group.

Ongoing client relations is a key block that exploits knowledge relating to each client and allows any consultant to ensure continuity in following up an urgent business request. A considerable amount of vital information sits in this database, called 'business': names, addresses and contact numbers, of course, the whole of previous correspondence – content of e-mails, telephone conversations, notes, documents exchanged, faxes received and sent, and so on. All this information is recorded, classified, indexed and archived. It becomes a complete file made up of a structured part and a non-structured part. This 'project' database is real knowledge capital especially during contracts with very large industrial or commercial groups, several departments of which in succession may call on this company's services.

In-depth work on the practical bringing together of knowledge exploitation methods and records management methods has made this knowledge management intranet more operational and more effective for the user. Information is organized according to the operating processes and handled according to the different security and storage levels (RM) and according to indexing techniques by authority list and as full-text recognizing the added value brought by each agent (KM).

Each client contract constitutes a separate information base of structured and non-structured information, which allows following up and sharing the whole of the project information, from the range of people and organizations involved to the most recent set of accounts, not forgetting project monitoring and project management tools. This project information, built on a permanent, homogeneous architecture, makes the same level of information available to each consultant at any time, whether they are in the office, on site with a client or on a train.

These databases are structured according to the classification of the sequence of processes in the business project itself, on several levels:

- Level 1: general indexing of every project with its description and associated clients
- Level 2: data of all types (e-mail, statistical data, documents, URLs, images, etc.) classified according to each business project's development process (for the project's quality assurance plan)
- Level 3: the non-variable data found in every project (project management data, daily log, project directory, documentation, invoice, contractual agreement, etc.)
- Level 4: each document is given a unique identifier in the form of a unique record number extended by its version number (for example: a report can be identified as 'company code + process code + project code + unique record number + version').

See this illustrated in Figures 10.2, 10.3 and 10.4.

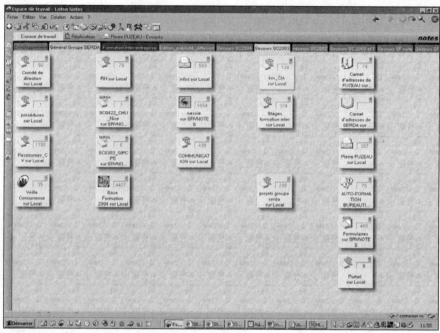

Figure 10.2   The work station

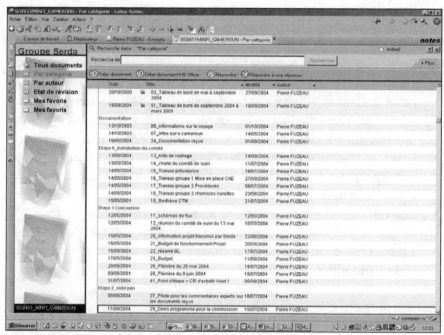

Figure 10.3   The work station

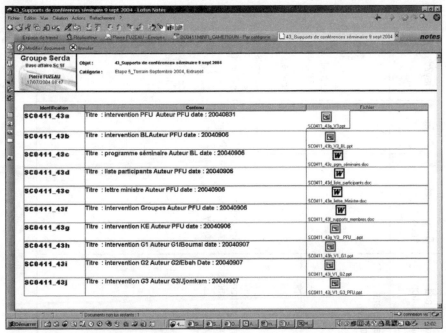

Figure 10.4   The work station

The intranet mind map

The intranet is full of information . . . and sometimes felt to be 'too full'. In late 2004 the need was felt for a mind map explaining the layers of knowledge. The mind map that emerged throws light on and gives useful reference points for every user to improve their contribution and to compensate for Lotus Notes' most cruel shortcoming: its lack of a horizontal search engine. See Figure 10.5.

Security

Without a high level security framework, the system of confidence in an intranet would be difficult to build up to a functional level. Each user would therefore tend to build up their own classification system in parallel to the intranet. For this reason the system was immediately designed with four security levels:

Intranet's relevant knowledge bases	Project management	Production	Marketing and communication	Documentation, knowledge	Project	Day2day
A C T I V I T I E S	Admin – general management	Management committee, procedures, CV resources, competitor intelligence	Management committee, HR, accounting	Management committee, infos			
	Consultancy	Specialist knowledge, processes	Business databases		Specialist knowledge, library		e-mail, transport, forms, address book, self-instruction, communication (internal)
	Customized training	CV resources, competitor intelligence		Communication, customer relations database, information			
	Standard training courses	Internal professional development training, processes, CV resources, competitor intelligence	Training/ production			Projects	
	Publications	Processes, CV resources, competitor intelligence	Desktop publishing				

Figure 10.5 Knowledge mind map

- Organizational and functional security: the only people with rights to make changes are the users directly involved in an activity; the only people with rights to delete are the project leaders or activity leaders. The mind map was used as the basis for security management.
- Hardware security and software security: Lotus Notes has proved itself as a robust platform and a back-up and replication system on a back-up platform has been set up on a number of distributed sites.
- A disaster plan in case of loss of or degraded functionality has been put in place and tested a number of times.
- Finally, periodic full back-ups (on NF Z 42-013 standards) are made on digital optical non-rewritable disks.

Results

The main difficulty encountered has been getting the work station adopted and used by each member of staff; sharing information and adding to the databases happened progressively with change being managed during the transitional phase (estimated duration three years). As the intranet increasingly proved its reliability, robustness and added value, users' confidence grew. It has to be said, however, that active support by the directorate had to be constant to help ensure this result. This permanent presence was based on teaching, management by example, communication of the directorate's intent and on evidence that the intranet functioned effectively.

The intranet has proved its reliability and it robustness (two or three complete interruptions of service of less than two hours in four years and putting the emergency system into action twice).

The intranet has also proved the high level of record tracking (when, who, what, access rights, and so on).

The hoped-for strong common culture did materialize. The result was a considerable increase in quality and homogeneity of response to clients (a reduction of about 70–80% of mistakes), an increase in the general level of competence in the teams taken as a whole and a productivity gain estimated in terms of time saved at between 20 and 30% (in some cases 50%).

The lessons to be learned from this case are that:

- The battle against individualism and differences in practice from department to department must be ongoing (is this peculiar to France?)

- A records management approach is absolutely essential to create the necessary climate of confidence to implement collaboration within the organization.
- A records management approach is not sufficient by itself but is the indispensable basis that needs to be complemented by knowledge management and business intelligence methods to increase expected benefits.

Conclusion

These two case studies relate to two very different kinds of organization, in terms of size and activity, but they are both in the private sector. The solutions adopted for managing electronic records differ significantly but both adopt a records management approach. They do, however, highlight common outcomes and lessons that can apply generically to organizations in the private sector where the emphasis is on customer satisfaction and maximization of profit. The focus on business classification and risk management and the key role of senior management support provide guidance and direction for organizations big and small.

Acknowledgement

This chapter was translated from the original French by Geoff Hare.

Chapter 11

Implementing a solution for electronic recordkeeping in the public sector

JUDITH ELLIS

Introduction

This chapter presents a case study from a city council in Australia. It shares how the council, having recognized the need for a long-term strategy for managing its records, adopted a knowledge management approach to implementing a solution. Five years on electronic recordkeeping is part of normal business processes and the success of the changes is due to the development of a sound and strategic framework, the people involved and the software deployed.

The business context
Introduction to Darebin City Council

The origins of local government in the area now occupied by Darebin City Council (DCC) started in 1854 with the proclamation of the Epping Roads Board. Various amalgamations and divestments and renaming of shires, boroughs, towns and cities within the region occurred regularly throughout its history, with the last major amalgamation of all or parts of five municipalities in 1994 when the City of Darebin was formed. The City now occupies 53 square kilometres of the inner northern suburbs of Melbourne, Australia. It includes 55,000 properties, 900 hectares of parkland, 5200 businesses and a population of 128,000 residents, with over one-third from countries other than Australia.

The Council owns a range of physical assets, including over 600 km of roads, 2000 km of drains, 300 buildings, 450 hectares of parkland and over 45,000 street trees. Its main industry sectors are manufacturing, retail, property and business services, with a small but rapidly expanding hospitality sector. The Council itself is the municipality's largest employer, with over 800 full- or part-time permanent staff and many more in casual positions (City of Darebin website www.darebin.vic.gov.au). It offers a range of services typical of local government in Australia: arts, culture and recreation; business and food health services; community health and safety; community services (aged, disability, family and children); customer service centres; disability access; environmental information; multicultural services; parking and transport; pets and local law enforcement; planning and building; public health information; rates and valuations; rubbish and recycling.

The Council's organizational structure has remained the same since the last major change in 2000. Headed by the Chief Executive Officer, the departments are: Asset Management, City Services, Community Services, Corporate Services, Culture and Leisure, Environment and Amenity, Strategy and Governance.

Background to the electronic recordkeeping initiative

In mid-1999 the Manager Executive Services and the Records Manager saw the need for a long-term records management strategy. Rather than focus on simply recasting the Registry and the distributed management of hard-copy files, they understood the need to incorporate the discipline of records management and the organization's recordkeeping practices into a wider, more strategic and relevant framework. What was needed was an enterprise-wide view, an approach to managing document-based information of all types, elimination of information silos and changes in individual and organizational behaviour.

A knowledge management approach was taken, involving a strategic framework to define the boundaries and projects, an external environmental analysis, business cases and plans, technology and information management tools to support the system infrastructure, culture-based initiatives, business process review and change, organizational development initiatives and definition of roles and responsibilities.

Stage 1 was to engage an external specialist consultancy firm to develop a knowledge management (KM) strategy and supporting business case, to undertake an information audit and to facilitate DCC's internal knowledge management team.

The business drivers for the KM programme were:

- delivering the highest possible value and service to stakeholders
- informed policy-making, decision-making and planning
- meeting corporate and internal accountabilities
- supporting DCC's leadership role
- enabling responsiveness and proactive action
- support of organizational core values of collaboration, accountability and respect
- maximizing return on human and other resources (City of Darebin, 2000b, 3).

The programme was linked to DCC's principles as articulated in its corporate plan, including good governance, accountability, responsiveness, leadership and learning, innovation and responsible resource management.

Electronic recordkeeping was an intrinsic part of this strategic approach. It was to enable responsive and timely access to, and management of, business-critical information to both internal and external customers. It contributed to the KM vision of:

> The generation and leverage of knowledge to enable Council to meet its business objectives and good governance in the creation of a diverse and democratic city where citizens work together to advance community life. This is done through the transformation of business process, infrastructure, and organizational culture to enable organizational responsiveness, adaptability, effectiveness and innovation.
>
> (City of Darebin, 2000b, 9).

Within only nine months of the KM initiative commencing, DCC had achieved:

- adoption of the KM Strategy and Business Case – involving 32 projects, and funding secured for the first year's implementation

- acceptance of the recommendations arising from the information audit
- establishment of a Council intranet, with the KM team home page as the pilot site, and appointment of a webmaster
- an ongoing best practice study involving a series of software briefings (e.g. electronic records and document management systems, portals and search engines), site visits for staff, presentations on case studies, collection of relevant resource material, hosting of an industry network for best practice research and development of a best-practice checklist
- development of an e-mail policy – the first of a series of recordkeeping standards
- regular issue of an internal KM bulletin
- participation in a university research study on knowledge management in local government
- industry showcasing by presenting at a national industry event
- implementation of a stage 1 communication plan, to inform staff about the KM strategy and promote involvement and commitment.

Stage 2 involved focusing on one major goal of the KM strategy – to provide electronic management of, and access to information throughout the Council. This was to be achieved by a major project to develop and implement a comprehensive electronic document and records management (EDRM) strategy over five years. A number of other projects fed into this one such as the intranet project, incorporation of informal hard copy records systems (in business units) into the existing records management database, electronic acquisition and storage of subscription-based resource material and development of a vital records programme.

The external specialist consultancy firm was retained to develop the EDRM system (EDRMS) strategy, which was subsequently adopted by management. Next came the development of a tender specification, acquisition method, product evaluation methodology, selection process, project plan, establishment of the project governance structure, and subsequent implementation.

The objectives of the EDRMS technology were to:

- enable a transition to an electronic office
- support DCC's electronic service delivery, e.g. e-business

- provide access to diverse and dispersed hard-copy document and records systems
- manage routine 'office' documentation, e.g. word-processed documents
- eliminate labour-intensive processes for hard-copy document management, e.g. file and correspondence management
- support the requirement for a workflow-enabled infrastructure
- support the management of the total customer interface, e.g. response to requests and complaints from outside
- enable risk management in information management.

(City of Darebin, 2000a, 6)

The resulting electronic recordkeeping framework covering technology, business rules, redesigned jobs and new work routines had commenced by late 2002, covering 350 staff and multiple locations. The EDRMS would replace the previous hard-copy records management systems.

The records and knowledge management function is now routinely recognized in DCC's annual report, which notes in particular the EDRM project, its integration with DCC's core systems, access to the system by remote users, and the effect on corporate memory with over 50,000 items being captured in its second year of operation.

Planning and policy framework
Governance

The governance framework for the EDRM project covered a number of levels, with roles and responsibilities clearly defined. Project ownership and sponsorship for the initial KM strategy (and resultant EDRM project) were vested in the senior executive team and the General Manager Corporate Services Department with the ultimate backing of the Chief Executive Officer.

At the next level a senior and cross-functional KM team was established. It comprised senior representatives from across the organization and was responsible for ensuring that the KM strategy, business case and resultant initiatives were tied to the business strategies and objectives of the Council, identifying opportunities or improved business process and infrastructure and promoting the KM initiative throughout DCC as a means of enabling its business drivers to be met. The KM team became the KM steering committee after the first year and met regularly to oversee the range of projects arising from the KM strategy, including the major EDRMS implementation. It reported to Council Executive.

An EDRMS project management team had primary operational responsibility for the EDRMS implementation. It comprised representatives from Information and Records Management, Information Systems (IS), and each of the departments. The role of this team was to develop the implementation plan, report on progress against the plan to the KM steering committee, to co-ordinate the focus groups in the implementation of various components of the project and to maintain communication with the organization about progress.

A series of focus groups reported to the project management team. Their role was to implement components of the project plan and report on progress. Their work was mostly short term, pre roll-out, and members of the groups were involved according to their specialist expertise and would change according to the project needs. Focus groups were established for system specification, system selection and acquisition, communication, staff development and cultural change, information management (design and rules) and implementation and installation – responsible for the planning and roll-out. Work was also being done throughout on IT infrastructure.

Following a restructure of Council administration, the Manager Executive Services was appointed as full-time Project Manager – Knowledge Management. She had been instrumental in the development of DCC's KM strategy and was made responsible for project managing the EDRMS implementation and co-ordinating all other KM projects. She held this position for three years until she left the organization.

The project team comprised the key six operational staff in the Records Management business unit of the Corporate Services Department. IS and Organization Development were also in this department.

In addition the following were implemented at other levels:

* A system (technical) manager – a senior database administrator in IS – was appointed.
* A system/application manager and a back-up person – these were the Records Manager and his second-in-charge – were appointed.
* Reporting responsibilities were defined.
* Responsibilities of operational staff were defined for those involved in implementation focus groups.

- No other internal roles were defined. The Organization Development Branch was not substantially involved.
- Contract negotiations identified the roles and responsibilities of the vendor. Fulfilment of the vendor project management role lacked continuity with three changes in personnel in three years.
- Records management staff position descriptions were revised to include their new roles of help desk, system administrator, user training, consultancy on EDRM solutions and issues.

Planning

The EDRMS project comprised five phases for the implementation of electronic recordkeeping from 2000 to 2005:

- development of strategy
- system specification
- selection and acquisition
- implementation (including design, configuration, testing, piloting and roll-out)
- maintenance and support.

The EDRM strategy had recommended a framework for the project management of the above, plus development of business rules, job redesign and change management. The results were:

- The project manager responsibilities were assigned to the Project Manager – Knowledge Management. A number of project team staff could assume some of her responsibilities if she was away.
- Jurisdictions and delegations were defined, e.g. for product selection, expenditure approvals, sign off on new business processes.
- Project reporting structures and methods were put in place.
- Other project staff were identified and roles and responsibilities defined.
- A very brief implementation plan was developed, mainly covering the training phases.
- A communication plan was developed (discussed further below).
- Various records management plans were developed, dealing with roll-out tasks, such as how to move from a paper-based environment to an electronic one.

- Key performance indicators (KPIs) were to be developed within the project plan for each sub-project. This was not done.
- Measurements to assess the benefits of the project were to be devised and implemented. This was not done in any structured way; however, there have been a number of indicators and reviews undertaken which have shown system usage and take-up.
- Culture and learning audits were to be done to assess employee understanding of changed work processes and the technology. This was done for the KM strategy.
- The deliverables and timeframes for each phase were met successfully.

The high-level business case for the EDRM had been defined by the KM strategy covering a three- to five-year period. A detailed capital works expenditure bid (equivalent of a business case) for the EDRM provided sufficient funding for the first two years of implementation. From then funding has been by annual recurrent budget allocations, covering items such as the yearly software maintenance and support agreement, salaries and other ongoing costs. Planned new initiatives such as OCR scanning will be subject to a capital works expenditure bid.

The EDRMS strategy identified critical project issues and dependencies for the project and the strategies for addressing those issues. For example, some critical project issues and dependencies included:

- project timetable not being met
- links with other projects
- availability of staff to undertake projects
- traditional processes and culture remaining
- availability of funding and other necessary resources
- demonstrated management commitment to the strategy
- ability to obtain user commitment and participation
- computing and network infrastructure problems.

Some mitigation strategies included:

- post-implementation review at each milestone or phase
- re-evaluation of project plan and resource allocation, and appropriate revision

- cross-representation on project teams to ensure co-operation, collaboration and effective deployment of resources
- buy-in of expertise or additional staff where required
- assessment of change management strategy and effectiveness of its implementation with revision as necessary
- project budgeting
- publicizing the successes
- phased implementation with immediate and visible benefits
- ensuring the overall strategy remained relevant to the Council operations
- sustaining management commitment
- ensuring ongoing project ownership
- demonstrating benefits
- training and communication
- devising a practical conversion/migration strategy.

Policy

An information management policy and standards document was issued during the EDRMS implementation for use by all staff. It purposely used generic language that the organization would understand, regardless of discipline. 'Information' was designated as a 'valuable resource . . . to be managed effectively to support Council's decision-making processes . . . to be captured in a manner that makes it accessible to all who need it, and managed in a way to ensure it is up to date' (City of Darebin, 2002, 1).

'Corporate information' was defined as 'any record (including documents, e-mails, database information) that is created or received by an officer in the course of his/her duties that forms part of the business activities of Council. Corporate information provides evidence of the Council's business activities and may be required for use by others or affect the work of others' (City of Darebin, 2002, 13).

This policy also outlined the roles and responsibilities of all staff, including operational staff, the management team, the Records Management Unit and the Information Services Branch (IS).

The standards covered basic rules for information (records) capture, official containers (repositories) for information, sharing information, security and confidentiality, legislative requirements and archiving and disposal of documents.

Electronic recordkeeping framework

In addition to the planning and policy framework outlined above, the electronic recordkeeping framework at DCC comprised three key elements:

- requirements analysis and definition
- selection and acquisition of leading-edge technology
- various implementation projects where outcomes were embedded into the system design and implementation.

DCC did not define document, records, information, data or the differences between them. As noted above it used the concept of 'corporate information' and defined it in a way that would normally apply to 'records'. This enabled the project to apply to all forms of content such as hard-copy documents, e-mails, images, web content, drawings and so on.

The EDRM initiative was also intended to link with other projects in DCC that might have recordkeeping implications, for example, implementation of the new graphical information system (GIS) and roll-out of remote computing to selected users.

Requirements definition

The analysis done for the EDRMS was based on the outcomes of the KM strategy, the information audit, analysis of the regulatory requirements and input from a range of stakeholders from the business areas. A detailed functional, technical and user specification was compiled and used as the basis for tendering, product evaluation, selection and acceptance testing. In summary the functional requirements included the following:

- integrated product, or proven integration with third-party products, for:
  - hard copy item management
  - electronic object management
  - workflow and workflow reporting
  - imaging
  - web-enabled access
  - reporting
- ability to meet regulatory and risk management requirements whereby the system must enable compliant and accountable electronic recordkeeping through:

- capture of documents as inviolate objects
- version and copy control
- provision of audit trails on documents and transactions
- security protocols for information access and for use of system functionality
- use of authority tables
- automatic disposal sentencing against online policy
- incorporation of government metadata systems
- transaction audit trails
- item capture, for example:
  - capture of all electronic information objects in any medium, any format and from any source, e.g. web documents, e-mail, electronic fax, digital images, maps, plans and drawings, and conversion and capture of hard-copy records in electronic form
  - capture at point of creation or receipt, rendering the object inviolate and unique
  - use of metadata schemes, e.g. thesauri, classification schemes
- hard-copy object management, for example:
  - item profiling
  - item tracking and barcoding
  - requests and resubmits
  - label printing
  - comprehensive search facilities
- electronic object management, for example:
  - version control
  - some level of auto-categorization, supported by document metadata systems
  - support of documents of various formats and 'item types'
  - online disposal
  - viewing of multiple document formats
  - comprehensive search facilities, including full-text search
  - enterprise-wide access from any location
- compliance with industry standards, for example:
  - AS4390 (since superseded by AS ISO 15489)
  - Victorian Electronic Records Strategy (VERS)
  - ODBC databases
  - industry standards for imaging and workflow, e.g. ODMA

- Relationship to core business systems, for example:
  - interface to designated core systems (e.g. GIS)
  - web content management.

System selection

The criteria for product selection were done on the basis of cost; vendor background and capability; level of support, maintenance and product development; technical fit and functional fit. A large range of people across the Council participated in the selection process, especially at the time of product demonstration and feedback, including general managers, representatives from business units, project team members and administrative staff. Products and vendors were initially shortlisted based on written tenders; on-site demonstrations against scripted requirements and a scenario for shortlisted products; additional technical, functional and contractual questions; reference site checks; an evaluation report; followed by selection of a single product or vendor. Prior to contract finalization a limited product trial was negotiated for simple user-testing of functionality, followed by full acceptance-testing. The entire process was open, clearly structured and highly consultative with the business.

Implementation

System implementation along with the related procedures and process changes started with some pilots, through introductory training to pilot groups and all designated champions across the organization, sessions to review pilot training and implementation and to act on lessons learnt, and advanced training for high-end users and champions. The rest of the implementation was phased, by grouping business units with strong interrelationships, and rolling out the preparatory design work, system installation, training and migration to each business unit. Roll-out took place at seven remote sites, such as shopfronts, depot, other services centres, as well as remote access for laptop users. The communications infrastructure was already in place for e-purchasing. In six months, 350 users were operational. The implementation strategy was not clearly defined at the outset, but the implementation process and peer pressure for take-up of the new technology meant that roll-out occurred quickly and relatively smoothly.

While the EDRM project took the focus and energies of management and staff away from the wider knowledge management initiative it was implemented according to the KM strategy. The EDRM project was a large, costly and culture-changing project and involved more than acquisition of technology. Various projects and activities were under way simultaneously and were being embedded into the EDRM implementation to provide a complete electronic recordkeeping infrastructure. For example:

- Small communities of practice were established to analyse and solve specific information management problems – thereby encouraging communication and collaboration.
- Various recordkeeping standards, business rules and policies were developed by the Information Management Focus Group and were built into EDRM system design and use. It developed the following for configuration and implementation of the system, as well as the training components to cover these areas:
  - definition of the compliance infrastructure, e.g. legislation, e-business requirements
  - classification scheme and rules for use
  - business rules
  - system design and parameters, e.g. object models, user definitions, security controls, folder structures, document naming conventions
  - metadata standards
  - standards for data/information ownership and custody (including external providers)
  - integration and interface requirements with Council core business systems such as the Property Database, the GIS, and e-mail system.
- Existing records disposal schedules were reviewed and loaded into the system but the disposal alert and action system has not yet been activated. This is a project for the next phase.
- Record creation, capture, storage, retrieval and access processes and employee behaviours were substantially revised, moving the organization from a central paper-based registry framework to a highly devolved, self-sufficient, electronic recordkeeping environment, regardless of employee location.

Clear decisions were made about document migration or conversion of existing or legacy collections. There was no back-capture of hard-copy documents except on the basis of need. Some 250,000 record entries from the previous records management system (used only for hard-copy records) were migrated to the new system, thus enabling ongoing access to legacy material. The legacy system was then decommissioned. Scanning of incoming hard-copy documents occurred from the designated 'go live' date onwards. Statistics show that more documents are being scanned and registered in the current system by the Records Unit than under the previous regime where many documents were simply forwarded by Records to the relevant line area for action, and not subsequently captured in any system. Users now receive the electronic record immediately after scanning.

In 2000 the tender process required vendors to state their ability to achieve compliance with the government's mandated Victorian Electronic Records Strategy (VERS). VERS was being designed as a whole-of-government standard for the identification, tagging and eventual storage of electronic records, which are considered archives of the state. Vendor capability in this area was unclear, despite their tender responses. Formal software product certification against the VERS standard had not yet commenced in the Victorian government at that time. However for Darebin it was a significant factor, as its strategy rested on the organization moving to an entirely electronic recordkeeping environment, including electronic archives. The product chosen is currently progressing through the stages of VERS certification.

The EDRMS has a very usable integration between it and DCC's GIS, which stores spatial information on properties. For example, the user can move easily between the EDRMS and the GIS to see geographical information about any property, and documents related to that property. This is used heavily by planning, valuations and rates business units.

Some core business systems are still used to capture related documents within those systems. For example invoices are captured within the purchasing system, response letters are captured within the property database. While the original intention was that the EDRMS would be used to capture all electronic records from all systems, the use of such business systems for capturing specific electronic records is clearly understood and presents no problems for users. As yet, there is no portal capability to search for records across all the different databases.

Web content management (WCM) was intended to be a component of the EDRMS; however, this has not yet been implemented using the current product, and DCC is currently in the process of selecting a point WCM solution.

Change management

Change management is critical in the implementation of new technologies especially where it will significantly alter the way people do their day-to-day work. For the electronic recordkeeping initiative this involved a change management strategy, a communication plan, training programmes and process change definition.

In accordance with the EDRM strategy, a range of change management and human resource programmes were implemented prior to, during and post system implementation:

- a training plan – determining the style, scope and delivery of a programme
- occupational health and safety assessments and definition of preventative or corrective action
- assessment of the requirement for temporary staff (e.g. data entry, scanning)
- change management – development of a strategy to manage cultural change, process changes, consultation and collaboration on new ways of working
- implementation of an organization-wide communication plan.

The communication plan was developed almost immediately after product selection, and covered the 12-month implementation period up to the system going live. Key features of this strategy were:

- the KM intranet site and a Records Unit intranet site became the key tools for communication to 800 staff
- project focus groups – during implementation
- various training and support programmes
- regular articles in the *Darebin Weekly Information Bulletin* on implementation progress
- regular Council information sessions and reports to Council meetings
- regular presentations and reports to the executive team, and involving them in choosing suitable pilot sites and roll-out priorities

- involvement of representatives from all business units in EDRM product demonstrations and selection
- use of the KM skills audit to introduce staff to the basic concepts of KM and EDRM
- availability of frequently asked questions (FAQ) sheets
- establishment of the help desk early in the process
- training refresher courses post-implementation
- individual assistance to units to improve business processes and folder structures
- surveys of users and focus groups to obtain feedback
- information on electronic recordkeeping included in staff induction programmes.

All user training was carried out by the Project Manager Knowledge Management and the Records Unit, and continues under the records staff. During the EDRMS implementation this included a customized user-training programme and staff received *Handy Hits Guide & Information Kit* and mouse pad with help desk details. In the last year 186 hours of EDRM training was delivered through introductory sessions and refresher sessions, and included almost 70 new employees.

Records staff also regularly attend departmental team meetings for discussion and consultation on the EDRMS, to clarify issues and to answer questions. In the last year they also held 65 EDRM consulting meetings, at the request of specific staff or business units to make better use of the system.

The EDRM strategy also recommended that a process change strategy be developed and implemented. This required:

- identification and mapping of process changes required
- redesign processes and workflows if relevant
- consultation and collaboration with staff
- implementation of process change with the system roll-out.

Benefits realization and outcomes
Assessment of benefits

The benefits of electronic recordkeeping and the specific implementation of an EDRM were articulated within the KM strategy and related business case. This placed the EDRM initiative within a wider, business-based and relevant context.

A number of reports and assessments have been undertaken to assess the progress, take-up and achievements of the electronic recordkeeping framework. For example, as part of DCC's 'Best Value' programme a baseline report was conducted less than one year into EDRMS implementation. The scope of the review included the EDRMS and the knowledge management function '(as) the Electronic Document Management System (EDRMS) is the foundation project of Darebin's Knowledge Management Strategy, and is being implemented according to knowledge management principles, it was considered beneficial to review the services together' (City of Darebin, 2003, 1). The Report recommended:

- Review of the Knowledge Management Strategy, including the future directions, resource requirements, new projects and priority for implementation of projects.
- Review of the strategy for the EDRMS roll-out including: fax gateway, scanning of drawings and plans, priorities for implementation for off-site locations, portal implementation.
- Determining the structure and framework required to use the (EDRM) workflow to automate business processes, including an evaluation of the resources required and process for implementation.
- Evaluation of the resources and processes required to carry out a vital records protection and archiving project to preserve hard copy documents.   (City of Darebin, 2003, 6)

In addition:

- The Records Management Unit regularly reports performance against key performance indicators as part of the service level agreement (SLA) that its parent department has with the rest of the organization.

- Regular monthly statistics are compiled and annually reported to senior management. These show increases (or decreases) in the number of electronic objects captured by the various departments, some showing up to a 950% increase in one year. These reports are used for management and the CEO to encourage use of the EDRMS, and publicizes higher level or refresher training.
- An annual 'achievements report' is compiled on the implementation of the system. This shows the volume of objects scanned into the system centrally, the extent of system training courses conducted, the number of consultations with business units seeking to make better use of the system, new uses and applications for the technology, enhancements to existing processes using the technology, upgrades and visits or briefings hosted for external organizations.

Outcomes

The EDRM project has fundamentally altered staff understanding and behaviour in relation to recordkeeping. There has been more than passive use of the system and conformance to business rules.

Adoption of electronic recordkeeping and use of the system have been positive. Peer pressure to use the technology and share and access information has resulted in an increase in the purchase of user licences. Staff are meeting the document naming standards and are saving documents appropriately within the system folder structure.

All hard-copy documents are received centrally and scanned. Hard-copy files are no longer created for most operations; staff access the electronic records and call for legacy hard-copy files for reference only. Some hard-copy files are still created for building and planning (e.g. planning-permit files) and registered in the EDRMS. Job application files and employee personal files were held in hard-copy form and managed by HR. This is currently changing to electronic capture and access, with electronic folders being established for these HR functions and protected by strong security protocols.

Business units have sought the assistance of the Records Unit in building specialized solutions (using the EDRMS) to assist their particular operations. For example: the establishment of electronic registers and processes for specific functions within Local Laws, Building, Planning Enforcement,

Health Services, Facilities Maintenance and Green Waste Collection Service and (at the request of the CEO) a register for Mayoral correspondence.

Results of regular monitoring are showing:

- Use of the EDRMS is increasing as people get used to the new routines.
- There is increased organizational push to use the system as people realize they need access to the complete story, not just part of it. This encourages people to capture records into the system as they see increasing value in sharing information and having quicker access to information.
- At the same time there is a need for persistence and reinforcement of the message for electronic recordkeeping.
- There is greater sharing of information, supported by the baseline rule that all records are open, other than by exception.

Effect on records management staff

The Records Management Unit took on complete responsibility for system administration, promotion, customization, user training and support for the EDRMS. In addition to many of their previous responsibilities, these staff now provide a range of higher level services to the Council, for example:

- development of recordkeeping strategies
- assistance in implementation of systems
- provision of user training and on going support
- development of short- and long-term information management strategies
- development of policies and standards
- planning and facilitating implementation
- provision of consultancy advice.

Records management staff consider the benefits to them are that:

- they are working with a leading technology product in local government
- they are having a say and input to the business of the organization, and now see themselves more as sayers not doers
- the project has raised their profile to 'information management', not just paper management

- they have significantly developed their skills, especially technical and training skills.

Achievements

The most significant achievements from the EDRM project are:

- The technology, business rules and support for electronic recordkeeping is almost self-sustaining.
- DCC has moved from a central hard copy Registry to a fully enterprise-wide, electronic office.
- While the entire framework will be under constant review, fine-tuning, upgrading and progressing, staff now operate within this framework as part of their normal business routine. Recordkeeping is not perceived as something separate or different from the business.
- The timing and continuity of strategy development, system selection, design and implementation has been a smooth process.
- There has been very little resistance to change, largely due to strong management support and good project management.
- The role, profile and competencies of records management staff have increased.
- Users come to the Records Unit with a business problem or issue to be solved. The electronic recordkeeping framework and technology are used to solve them and improve business processes.
- There is continued strong management support.

At a corporate level DCC is a showcase for this project:

- It has provided a positive image for DCC, and has management recognition.
- DCC hosts many visits or briefings each year from other organizations around Australia, and gives e-mail advice to overseas organizations.
- It is a good reference site for the EDRMS vendor.
- The case study has been published in industry magazines and presentations made to industry groups.
- The Council initiated and led a KM community of practice in LG Pro – the peak body for local government professionals in Victoria.

Challenges and lessons learnt

The main challenges for the project were:

- the low level of computing skills in some areas
- the need for strong partnership with IS
- a long period between selecting the product and the start of the implementation process, which took six months owing to contract negotiations, initial inadequate vendor project management, and the requirements for some of the integration functionality to be fully tested and working
- the level of demand on the Records Unit was underestimated, (eventually one extra staff member was engaged for a short period, which helped considerably)
- how to get the system design right. It was done as simply as possible for usability and take-up but some slight changes could have made it even simpler without loss of functionality.

In hindsight a number of additional tasks may have assisted or improved the outcomes. A stakeholder analysis would have indicated how to identify and manage particular stakeholders, where potential support or resistance lay, and which groups to include in the decision-making process. This knowledge could have been integrated into the strategic and operational management process.

Use of a formal project management methodology would have provided a more structured framework of governance, budget management and scheduling; however, the project did not suffer from a lack of such a methodology.

A post-implementation assessment on whether the objectives of the KM strategy or EDRMS strategy were being met would ensure that the outcomes and ongoing implementation still aligned with DCC's strategic objectives and business drivers for the project. Some metrics comparing pre- and post-implementation recordkeeping routines might provide some insight into the organization's business efficiency, for instance in customer management.

The design of a formal monitoring and compliance framework would enable the Records Unit and management to assess gaps in recordkeeping practice and opportunities for improvement.

Conclusion

The transition to electronic recordkeeping was part of a wider strategy linked to DCC's core business objectives. Five years on, the next strategic step is to review how far the Council has achieved and continues to achieve its knowledge management objectives including electronic recordkeeping. The next phase of the EDRM project has commenced with plans to:

- conduct a post-implementation review; this will include review of what electronic records are stored on network drives (instead of the EDRMS) and assessment of user take-up
- re-engineer and redesign some work processes with the introduction of workflow
- use OCR scanning to improve the level of metadata tagging of scanned objects
- design and embed the required functionality into the technology to enable electronic and automated records disposal
- use the web publishing function of the EDRMS to send content to DCC's new web content management system
- undertake a major drawings management project – using the EDRM to link and store the complex layers, formats and versions of internal and external drawings used by the Council, including the 10,000 legacy drawings already captured in the system.

Electronic recordkeeping is how normal business is done at the City of Darebin. In just over five years the organization has moved from a traditional, paper-based, central registry, typical of local government in Australia, to an organization that perceives clear business benefits from its enterprise-wide and robust electronic recordkeeping infrastructure. A number of fundamental changes have occurred: the increased capabilities, role and profile of the Council's records staff; best-of-breed records management technology; self-sufficient operational staff in the capture, retrieval and re-purposing of information; and sound business rules embedded into electronically driven recordkeeping routines.

Darebin City Council attributes this success to the initial development of a sound and strategic framework, an excellent and dynamic internal Project Manager, a high level of senior and middle level management support throughout, the positive attitude and competence of the Records

Unit – ready to embrace, encourage and support change – and selection of a leading-edge software product to underpin the electronic recordkeeping framework.

References

City of Darebin website, www.darebin.vic.gov.au [accessed 1 September 2005].

City of Darebin (2000a) EDMS Strategy – Knowledge Capture and Access via the Corporate Electronic Document Management System (unpublished), Darebin, Darebin City Council.

City of Darebin (2000b) KM 2000+ A Strategy for the Generation and Leverage of Knowledge Beyond 2000 (unpublished), Darebin, Darebin City Council.

City of Darebin (2002), Information Management Policy and Standards (unpublished), Darebin, Darebin City Council.

City of Darebin (2003), Best Value Baseline Report, Records and Knowledge Management (unpublished), Darebin, Darebin City Council.

City of Darebin (2004) *For the Record: annual report 2003–2004*, Darebin, Darebin City Council.

Chapter 12

Playing the long game – creating and maintaining the links in the value chain

JULIE McLEOD AND CATHERINE HARE

Introduction

Much has been written about the challenges of managing electronic records and the chapters in this book have aimed to address them. The nature of the records themselves and the tools to manage them present three challenges. First, in managing e-records we are dealing with objects that are intangible, whose value is not always acknowledged, and in an environment that is virtual and dynamic. Second, the tools we use are dynamic and constantly evolving as indeed are the solutions. And third, the tools themselves at best do not give priority to recordkeeping and at worst create nightmares for records managers. 'Deleted' records that remain recoverable and storage media that survive but become inaccessible, because the hardware and software to read them have disappeared, are but two examples.

We are, therefore, faced not only with keeping pace with new ICTs and learning how to use them but also with understanding their implications for and impact on recordkeeping. A danger in this dynamic environment is to focus on the tools rather than what they are creating and what needs to be managed and, in the process, losing sight of where we are trying to get to, indeed of where we need to be. We could address the immediate management problems with an IT solution by implementing a software tool. However, since information is the lifeblood of many organizations we must ensure we do not lose the value of the information that is contained in records and add value by managing and exploiting it. How can we achieve this?

The case studies presented by Judith Ellis and Pierre Fuzeau demonstrate that there is no single best solution, one size does not fit all. What they do show is that records management is a management activity and, like all management activities, the approach needs to address the strategic, tactical and operational levels. The contributors to this book have offered frameworks, advice and guidance that address all three levels.

As well as needing to cover these three levels, the successful management of e-records is not something that can be achieved overnight in the form of a once and for all solution. This is the long game. An exciting one, a scary one, a combination of the known and unknown, and one in which we need to be key players but where we need to work with teams with complementary skills, to play and win the game.

In the opening chapter John McDonald set the scene. He offered the following suggestions for accelerating positive change and tackling the management of e-records:

- establishing a vision
- enhancing awareness
- assigning accountability
- designing an architecture
- building capacity.

And he emphasized that achieving these goals is impossible without leadership.

Taking these ideas as a starting point, our aim in this final chapter is to draw together the fundamental points raised by each of the contributors, and therefore all of the key aspects of managing e-records, and propose a generic framework for the long and potentially never-ending game.

A generic framework for e-records management

Throughout the chapters all of the authors have highlighted that managing e-records successfully involves everyone in the organization and/or society – the task is enormous. Verne Harris puts the South African example into a wider international context and conveys this message by arguing that electronic recordkeeping must always be understood within the broader organizational and societal contexts or else any attempts to promote sound e-recordkeeping are doomed to failure. He also suggests that, ultimately, this is a matter of politics and that getting the politics right brings in the question of ethics.

But what is different? Has this not always been the case? Yes, but while the goals may be similar, the mechanisms and the environment in which it takes place are different and the challenges are different.

In the industrial era where records supported the business of organizations their management was the preserve of the few and was determined by time and space. In the electronic environment where records are no longer physical items and everyone has a role in their management, although not always understanding that role, the classical challenges still remain and need to be actioned. However, in addition to doing the same things, often in new ways, there are new things to be done. These are only achievable by understanding the whole, putting in place the appropriate environment and then doing it. Good intentions are not enough (Schwartz, n.d.).

The framework we offer to move forward, to plan and play the long game comprises the essential elements that have emerged from the content of the book but presented at the three management levels. They include vision and leadership, awareness and understanding, the environment, infrastructure and architecture, technical solutions, people issues and the things to be done.

The strategic level

Establishing the vision has to be the starting point and the vision has to focus on doing the right things. These must be business driven – based on the organization's goals, and process driven rather than records driven. The focus needs to be on ensuring that the activities, processes and transactions of the organization are recorded so that the full, authentic and fixed evidence and information are available to support business operations and meet legal requirements. So, while e-records management may not be a strategic function or activity in itself it must be aligned with the organization's strategic functions, activities and goals, be they financial and profit driven, customer service driven, or culturally driven.

Nowhere is this more powerfully illustrated than in Judith Ellis's case study of Darebin City Council presented in the previous chapter. From the outset the Council took a long-term, strategic approach to e-recordkeeping, driven by the business needs, and embedded it within a wider, more strategic and relevant knowledge management framework. This approach, together with a dynamic project manager, competent records professionals and a high level of management support, means that in a little over five years e-recordkeeping is how normal business is done in the Council.

It will be important to link the e-records strategy with other strategies, such as IT, information, risk management and corporate governance, and not isolate it. John McDonald quotes the example of the Canadian Government's policy on the management of government information. And Hans Hofman highlights the role that the ISO 15489, the international records management standard, can play at the level of policy and engagement with the business and its leaders.

Knowing where you want to be is crucial but, as John McDonald points out, getting there will be impossible without leadership. Where should that come from? Certainly records managers need to be leaders but their voice is unlikely to be strong enough on its own. Leadership also need to come from senior management and/or other allies at other levels in the organization. Pierre Fuzeau in the second of his case studies from the French private sector identifies senior management support and active involvement and commitment as key success factors in successful management of e-records.

The tactical level

Key facets of this level are the people and the environment including the infrastructure. Awareness and understanding on the part of records creators and users about the need to manage electronic records in the particular organizational context are vital. But this is not all – it needs to be followed by action. What is the nature of their task? What do they need to do, how, when and where? What are they responsible for, what are they accountable for and to whom? Understanding this begins by increasing and enhancing awareness and, as Thijs Laeven and David Ryan discuss, continues with training.

So we see that there are a number of players. There are the specialists such as the records management professionals, IT and systems administrators; the general strategists such as the executives and managers; and finally everyone. All involved need to work together, forming partnerships, recognizing and being equipped with the necessary knowledge and skills for their various roles and continuing to learn and update. Thijs Laeven underlines the importance of establishing competency frameworks, focusing in particular on records management professionals and emphasizing the contribution they should be making at the strategic level. He also explains the desirability of continuous professional development because understanding is not a one-off event but needs to be maintained.

But the people can only be effective in their recordkeeping roles if they are provided with the appropriate environment. This comprises not only the systems and technologies – the technical infrastructure – but also the other components of the records management infrastructure – the policies, standards, tools and practices, as well as the skilled and competent human resources.

Several of the chapters address different components of the infrastructure. Hans Hofman considers the range of standards – national, international, *de facto* industry standards – that can be adopted to support the implementation of effective recordkeeping. Kate Cumming examines why good metadata enables good records management and how, from a wider perspective, its effective application can help an organization achieve its broader objectives, such as better information access and greater accountability. To do this it must be implemented in appropriate systems in a considered manner, and Cumming explores a number of practical strategies for metadata implementation.

Also at the tactical level is the issue of preservation and this is covered in different ways in two chapters. First, David Ryan takes an organizational view of the challenge of digital preservation by considering its purposes and context, and gives practical advice on setting up a digital preservation business unit where one is required. He highlights a critical issue in this context, which he believes is not yet well understood and a cause for serious concern. This is that to have determined management of electronic records requires an understanding of what the benefits are compared with the costs over an extended period of time.

Richard Marciano and Reagan Moore complement David Ryan's chapter by looking at the technical aspects of archival preservation in the digital environment. They examine the technologies that aid the creation of preservation environments as mechanisms for managing the preservation material independently of the choice of storage or database technology. In doing so they refer to a number of practical examples and ongoing research coupled with the use of standards and the role of metadata referred to in Chapters 2 and 3.

The preservation process must preserve the authenticity and integrity of the records and the law's requirement that organizations be able to demonstrate that their electronic and other recordkeeping systems are operated with integrity is just one of several legal issues explored by David Stephens. Records and information specialists have a key role to play in the authenticity and integrity of business records in the 'corporate' environment that is ever more open to scrutiny in light of scandals of poor corporate governance.

The operational level

While implementation inevitably has strategic and tactical dimensions, its real focus is at the operational level. Things that need to be done at this level include:

- review and assessment of the current environment
- risk analysis
- creation, capture and organization
- application and deployment of metadata, development of fileplans
- implementation of preservation strategies
- maintaining staff understanding and awareness
- embedding records management into the day-to-day normal operations – the business processes.

It is also important to keep a careful watch on technology developments and not forget to consider continuous improvement – reviewing and refining the implementation of the vision.

The case studies highlight how different approaches have worked well for different organizations and their needs at the operational level. Several other chapters have referred to examples and sources of practical advice and guidance useful at the operational level. There is no ready-made generic blueprint but there is practice that is transferable. The key is to act and do things right at this level.

Revolution through evolution

But there will always be room for improvement and refinement. New solutions will be developed and systems will evolve. Our depth of understanding will increase as we gain more and more experience. Research and development will lead to and inform evidence-based practice. The benefits of the global ICTs that make possible global alliances and research projects, such as those reviewed by Xiaomi An, the work presented by Richard Marciano and Reagan Moore, and the work referenced by Hans Hofman, will make sure that the dissemination and application of best practice takes on an international dimension

Conclusion

There is much to do in relation to the current environment and in anticipation of future requirements and future environments. The temptation is to think that the task is too big and therefore to focus on one aspect at the expense of others. But we have to think holistically – no one else will. Also we have to do something and not be overawed into stagnation, avoiding the 'paralysis by analysis' situation, while recognizing that we are working with a moving target.

We need to learn to live with discomfort and imperfection, be comfortable with change and uncertainty. Did we achieve perfection in the physical, paper world? Hardly. So why should we strive for perfection and doing it 'right first time' in the digital world? If we wait for the perfect solution we risk losing the records or having such a legacy of ill-managed records that we cannot apply the solution retrospectively. But we need to be wary of the magic bullet solution provided by some software suppliers who focus on the solution to the business problem. For example, e-mail 'archiving' software keeps all e-mails, provides sophisticated retrieval and keeps the purchaser locked in by requiring ever bigger storage devices, rather than providing a recordkeeping solution that would solve retrieval and exponential storage problems by identifying those e-mails that are records and keeping only them for as long as they are needed and no longer.

We must work to close the good intentions gap (Schwartz, n.d.) and ensure that the good ideas are actually carried through to the real world. Some compromises with best practice may be necessary but best intentions do not matter – results do.

Coming back to the need for a vision and the need to exploit the value of information, as indicated in the introduction to this chapter, we can adopt a meaningful mantra encapsulated in the word VALUE, with its idea of a value chain, to provide guidance and a persistent point of reference and review. The links in the chain spell out the word as follows:

Vision
Awareness, action and accountability
Leadership
Us, you and users
Environment, education, expertise and empowerment

The case studies are testament to this framework and acronym or mantra. Playing the long game at the strategic level needs vision and leadership to heighten the chance(s) of success. At the tactical level it means awareness, the right environment (appropriate systems infrastructure and good information architecture), user education and expertise to build capacity. It involves all of us. And the operational level demands action by empowered and accountable people using systems and procedures.

We are not on our own. Technology has served us well by making it easier to share, by making available material from governments, national archives and other bodies and groups in the form of practical guidance and advice, expertise and real experience. One of the drivers for publishing this book was to collate and share current thinking, expertise and experience and to provide support for each other in playing a 'game' that is real, for which the rules are not all written, that has short-term as well as long-term goals, and that is challenging but has the potential for a good result.

Today's solutions are not necessarily long-term ones, even if they are part of the play for the long game. So, we need the energy, mental capacity and appropriate frame of mind to cope and live with the dynamic environment. If not then we risk not taking the bumpier, less travelled road, as David Ryan describes it, which is the road we need to take if we are to succeed. Whatever the course of our journey, above all, and to paraphrase Samuel Taylor Coleridge, we need a willing suspension of disbelief in our future uncertain and imperfect electronic world, and to have faith in our ability to succeed.

Reference

Schwartz, M. The Good-Intention Gap: records management realities,
www.itcinstitute.com/display.aspx?ID=139 [accessed 1 September 2005].

Index